HOW TO BE
COMPASSIONATE

His Holiness the
Dalai Lama

HOW TO BE COMPASSIONATE

A Handbook for Creating
Inner Peace and a Happier World

Translated from Oral Teachings and Edited by
Jeffrey Hopkins, Ph.D.

ATRIA PAPERBACK
NEW YORK   LONDON   TORONTO   SYDNEY   NEW DELHI

ATRIA PAPERBACK
A Division of Simon & Schuster, Inc.
1230 Avenue of the Americas
New York, NY 10020

Jeffrey Hopkins, Ph.D., is the translator into English and editor of the original oral Tibetan materials.

First Atria Paperback edition December 2011

ATRIA PAPERBACK and colophon are trademarks of Simon & Schuster, Inc.

For information about special discounts for bulk purchases, please contact Simon & Schuster Special Sales at 1-866-506-1949 or business@simonandschuster.com.

The Simon & Schuster Speakers Bureau can bring authors to your live event. For more information or to book an event, contact the Simon & Schuster Speakers Bureau at 1-866-248-3049 or visit our website at www.simonspeakers.com.

Manufactured in the United States of America

10   9   8   7   6   5

Library of Congress control no. for the hardcover edition: 2011281813

ISBN 978-1-4516-2390-1
ISBN 978-1-4516-2391-8 (pbk)
ISBN 978-1-4516-2392-5 (ebook)

Contents

Contents

Foreword

When the Chinese Communist government in Beijing hears that His Holiness the Dalai Lama has been invited to visit a country, it immediately files an objection with that nation's leaders, who all too often then find his visit to be inconvenient, or downscale the visit, or make it "personal." What do Chinese officials fear? The Dalai Lama has no army, no economic power, and no political cards to play. He advocates nonviolence and compassion. What do they fear?

The Chinese Communist government in Beijing offered to negotiate with His Holiness anywhere at any time, so long as the Dalai Lama did not bring up the topic of Tibetan independence. He has not raised that topic since 1978, but still, the response from Beijing has been to make all sorts of conditions. What do they fear?

His Holiness the Dalai Lama has inspired the

rebuilding of Tibetan cultural institutions outside of Tibet. He has asked the religious and political leaders of the world to look beyond their narrow interests to the greater good. He has advocated paying attention to the basic needs of all people, regardless of religion or politics—placing an emphasis on compassion and kindness. Is this what is feared?

Unlike Mao, who said power comes from the barrel of a gun, the Dalai Lama says the greatest power comes from compassion in your heart—the power to gradually create harmony and peace throughout the world. In Tibetan, and increasingly in English, he speaks with breadth, depth, intelligence, humor, and sincerity that inspire insight and motivate people to dedicate themselves to the welfare of others. I believe that he has inspired more people to work together with him on more books than any leader in world history.

In this brief book, I have gathered essential teachings of this world-renowned leader, whose message—that compassion is essential for individuals and for the world—is as renowned as the bearer himself. When we think of the Dalai Lama, we immediately think of the compassion he embodies, to which he has devoted his entire life.

In these pages, he calls us to pay attention to our own hearts—to our orientation to everyone and everything around us. His Holiness points out mistakes of attitude, how we make them, and how we can correct them for a better future. He begins by explaining how caring for others can be a profound source of happiness on an individual level, which can then be extended outward in wider and wider circles. Then, in nine subsequent chapters, he describes basic mistakes that lead to personal turmoil and interpersonal disruption, along with solutions for these problems. He focuses on the nature of hatred, because of its central role in undermining our potential for unbounded compassion, and then asks us to examine the nature of consciousness so that we understand how transformation of attitude is possible. This leads to three chapters on how to implement compassion in daily life, and a final chapter of heartfelt advice on how to live with greater and greater care and concern for all beings.

The Dalai Lama's full name, translated from Tibetan into English syllable by syllable, is "Leader, Holiness, Gentleness, Renown, Speech, Dominion, Mind, Goodness, Primordial, Wisdom, Teaching, Hold, Vastness, Ocean, Being, Triad, Controlling, Unparalleled, Glory, Integrity." (Tibetan: *rJe btsun 'jam dpal ngag dbang blo bzang ye shes bstan 'dzin rgya mtsho srid gsum dbang bsgyur mtshungs pa med pa'i sde dpal bzang po.*) Here is a poem I wrote in the mid nineteen-seventies, inspired by the Dalai Lama's name.

> *Leader* of the world recognized for true *holiness*,
> *Gentleness* personified in persuasive *renown*,
> *Speech* of compassion pervading the planet in its *dominion*,
> *Mind* of altruistic endeavor reaching all in its *goodness*,
> *Primordial* in the depth and range of profound *wisdom*,
> *Teaching* encompassing all phenomena in its *hold*,
> *Vastness* of love's deeds rippling throughout life's *ocean*,
> *Being* so merciful displayed in suffering's *triad*,
> *Controlling* the unruly through kindness *unparalleled*,
> *Glory* in forms of endeavor sealed in total *integrity*,
> May the teacher of the world, bearing compassion
> And wisdom indissoluble, see all obstacles dissolve.

Throughout the thirty-nine years that I have known the Dalai Lama and during the ten that I served as his chief translator on lecture tours in the United States, Canada, Indonesia, Singapore, Malaysia, Australia, Great Britain, and Switzerland, I have witnessed how he embodies compassion to the very core of his being. It is important for us to recognize that this insightful, compassionate, humorous, and marvelous person rose from Tibetan culture. We need to value that culture as one of the world's great wonders.

Tibetan culture extends far beyond Tibet, stretching from Kalmyk Mongolian areas near the Volga River (in Europe where the Volga joins the Caspian Sea), Outer and Inner Mongolia, the Buryat Republic of Siberia, Bhutan, Sikkim, Ladakh, and parts of Nepal. In all of these areas, Buddhist ritual and scholastic studies are conducted in Tibetan. Youths came from throughout these vast regions to study in Tibet, especially in and around its capital, Lhasa, but also throughout its three provinces, usually returning to their own lands after completing their studies (until Communist takeovers in many of these countries).

This highly accessible book, made so by the Dalai Lama's long fascination with science and his three decades of interacting with international scientists, draws from a long tradition of Tibetan techniques for transformation of mind and heart, reminding us of the importance of maintaining a homeland for its preservation. The light shining through His Holiness Dalai Lama's teachings has its source in that marvel of spiritual culture, offering insights and practices that we and the world so sorely need.

Jeffrey Hopkins, Ph.D.
Emeritus Professor of Tibetan Studies
University of Virginia

Introduction: Recognizing the Source of Happiness

Our lives are in constant flux, which generates many predicaments. However, when these are faced with a calm and clear mind supported by spiritual practice, they can all be successfully resolved. By contrast, when our minds are clouded by hatred, selfishness, jealousy, and anger, we not only lose control, we lose our sense of judgment. At those wild moments, anything can happen. Our own destructive emotions pollute our outlook, making healthy living impossible. We need to cleanse our own internal perspective through the practice of wise compassion.

When you are caught up in a destructive emotion, you have lost one of your greatest assets: your independence. At least for the time being, your mind is disturbed, which weakens your capacity for sound judgment. In the grip of strong lust or hatred, you forget to analyze whether an action is suitable, and can even speak crazily and make wild gestures. Afterward, when that emotion fades, you often end up embarrassed and sorry for what you have done. This shows us that, while you had fallen under the influence of that strong emotion, your capacity to distinguish between good and bad, between suitable and unsuitable, was nowhere to be found.

Although unfavorable conditions need to be removed, when they are removed with hatred, the means of relief creates its own problems, because hatred, distorted by its bias, does not see the true situation. But unfavorable conditions can be removed through analysis—by examining the facts and discerning the actual situation—without any negative emotional side effects.

Only human beings can judge and reason; we understand consequences and think in the long term. Human beings also can develop infinite love, whereas animals have only limited forms of affection and love. However, when humans become angry, all this potential is lost. No enemy armed with mere weapons can undo these qualities, but anger can. It is the destroyer. When animals act out of lust or hatred, they do so temporarily or superficially; they are incapable of committing destruction in ever-increasing strength and variety. However, humans can think from a great many points of view. Because our intelligence is so effective, humans can achieve good and bad on a grand scale.

When we look deeply into such things, the blueprint for our actions can be found within the mind. Self-defeating attitudes arise not of their own accord but out of ignorance. Success, too, is found within ourselves. From self-discipline, self-awareness, and clear realization of the defects of anger and the positive effects of kindness, come happiness and peace. For instance, at present, you may be a person who gets easily irritated. However, with clear understanding and awareness, your irritability first can be undermined, and then replaced.

If we allow love and compassion to be dominated by anger, we will sacrifice the best part of our human intelligence—wisdom, which is our ability to decide between right and wrong. Along with selfishness, anger is one of the most serious problems facing the world today. Anger plays a large role in current conflicts, such as those in Asia, the Middle East, and Africa, as well as those between highly industrialized and economically undeveloped nations. These conflicts arise from a failure to understand how much we have in common.

Answers cannot be found in the development and use of greater military force, nor can they be purely political or technological. The problems we face cannot be blamed upon one individual person or a single cause, for they are the result of our own negligence. What is required is an emphasis on what we have in common. Hatred and fighting cannot bring happiness to anyone, even to those who win. Violence always produces misery, so it is fundamentally counterproductive.

How can a world full of hatred and anger achieve real happiness? If we examine our long history of turmoil, we see the obvious need to find a better way. Attempts by global powers to dominate one another through arms races—whether nuclear, chemical, biological, or conventional—are clearly counterproductive. The sale of weapons, thousands and thousands of types of arms and ammunition by manufacturers in big countries, fuels the violence, but more dangerous than guns or bombs are hatred, lack of compassion, and lack of respect for the rights of others. External peace is impossible without inner peace. As long as hatred dwells in the human mind, real peace is impossible. We can only solve our problems through truly peaceful means—not just peaceful words, but actions based on a peaceful mind and heart. This is the way we will come to live in a better world.

On every level, the most mischievous troublemakers we face are anger and egoism. The kind of egoism I refer to here is not just a sense of "I," but an exaggerated self-centeredness that leads to manipulating others. As long as anger dominates our disposition, we have no chance of achieving lasting happiness. In order to achieve peace, tranquility, and real friendship, we must minimize anger and cultivate kindness and a warm heart. As we become nicer human beings, our neighbors, friends, parents, spouses, and children will experience less anger, prompting them to become more warm-hearted, compassionate, and harmonious. The very atmosphere becomes happier, which even promotes good health. This is the way to change the world.

It is time for all of us, including world leaders, to learn to transcend differences of race, culture, and ideology in order to regard each other with appreciation for our common human situation. To do so would uplift individuals, families, communities, nations, and the world at large.

Those countries that have achieved great material progress are beginning to understand that the condition of society, and of our physical well-being, is closely related to our state of mind. This is where profound change has to begin. Individually, we have to work to change the basic perspectives on which our feelings depend. We can only do so through spiritual training, by engaging in transformative practice with the aim of gradually reorienting the way we perceive others and ourselves.

THE NEED FOR COMPASSION AND TOLERANCE

There are different levels of happiness. Physical happiness is often related to material things, whereas mental happiness stems from inner or spiritual development. Since our sense of self, or "I," contains dual aspects—physical and mental—we need to address both. Balancing them is crucial to the good of human society.

Schemes for world development arise from our basic urge to attain happiness and relieve suffering. But just as we need a long-range perspective to protect our external environment, we need an internal strategy that extends far into the future. It is noble to work at external solutions, but they cannot be successfully implemented so long as our minds are ruled by anger and hatred. Living in society, we must share the suffering of our fellow citizens, and practice compassion and tolerance toward our enemies as well as our loved ones.

We must set an example by our own actions, for mere words cannot convince others of the merit of our values. We must live by the same high standards of integrity and sacrifice we seek to convey to others. This requires moral strength. The ultimate purpose of compassionate values is to serve and benefit the world. This is why it is so important that we always aim to promote the happiness and peace of *all* beings. For this, we need transformative practice.

In life we are confronted by unfavorable circumstances, one after another, day in and day out. By simply reacting, we generate counterproductive emotions, specifically lust, hatred, and confusion, which produce even more suffering in the future. Those who reject transformative practice generally do not see lust and hatred as problematic; instead of viewing these destructive emotions as toxic, they allow themselves to be controlled by these attitudes. Those who do choose transformative practice, however, view lust and hatred as emotions to be avoided and, for the most part, these people are more peaceful, and happier.

I question the popular assumption that ethics has no place in politics, and that spiritually minded people should sequester themselves from the ways of the world. Such a view lacks a proper perspective on the individual's relation to society, and the role of compassionate values in our lives. Religions themselves often call for giving up attachment to the world, but this does not mean that you can no longer be an agent for positive change.

In 1954, I travelled to Beijing to meet with Mao Zedong. During our final meeting in 1955, he told me, "Religion is poison for two reasons. The first is that it harms development of the nation. The second is that it diminishes the population." His thought was that if many people became monastic, it would reduce the number of births. In hindsight, we can say now that more monastics are just what China needed to reduce overpopulation! Mao simply did not understand the real meaning of religion. He did not know that the essence of religion is caring and concern for others.

Ethical behavior is just as crucial to a politician as it is to a religious practitioner. Dangerous consequences follow when politicians and rulers forget moral principles. Whether we believe in God or karma (the power of actions and their effects), strong ethical values are the foundation of society, and must become the underpinning of our daily lives. Still, the good intentions of various religions and philosophies are not sufficient; we must implement them day by day in social interaction. Then we can realize the full value of these teachings.

When you generate a well-founded aspiration to enhance the happiness of others, you become more humane. The ultimate purpose of transformative mental practice is to help others. In order to do so, you must remain in society, contributing according to your ability. As you develop inwardly, you can contribute outwardly with greater force.

COUNTERACTING DESTRUCTIVENESS

We all want happiness and do not want suffering, and since the pain we seek to avoid mainly stems from twisted mental attitudes, we have to consider whether there are any forces that oppose these destructive emotions. If, for instance, anger causes suffering, then we must find its antidote. The antidote for anger is compassion. Anger and compassion are both attitudes, but they have contradictory ways of seeing the same object. Their outlooks are exactly opposite.

If a room is too hot, the only way to reduce the heat is to introduce cold. Just as heat and cold oppose each other, so, too, do mental states such as anger and compassion. To the extent you develop one, the other decreases. This is the way that counterproductive states of mind are reduced, and finally removed. Antidotes exist, and must be found and introduced.

To help you in your effort to resolve your own problems, picture yourself as a sick person who has come under the influence of three destructive diseases: lust, hatred, and ignorance. Transformative practices are like medicines, acting in opposition to these internal ailments. The practice of compassion is like a remedy for ruinous overemphasis on your self.

The sole source of peace within you, in the family, the country, and the world, is altruism—love and compassion. At the core of our existence as human beings is the desire to live purposeful, meaningful lives. Our purpose is to develop a warm heart. We find meaning in our lives by being a friend to everyone. Altruism is the cure because it is the authentic way to conduct your life.

HOW TO HELP

We need to base our lives on altruistic concern, aimed not just at our own private welfare but also at the good of society. As I have mentioned, if people could enjoy both external prosperity and inner qualities of goodness, that indeed would provide a comfortable human life. Therefore, we need to engage in activities for the welfare of the world as a whole, such as building schools, hospitals, and factories. However, since happiness mainly derives from inner attitudes, helping others should not be limited to providing food, shelter, and clothing, but must also include replacing the *basic* causes of suffering with the *basic* causes of happiness.

Just as smart public policy aims to educate people so that they can take care of their own lives, so it is with the practice of altruism: the most effective way to help others is by teaching them what to adopt in their future practice and what to discard from their current behavior. People need to learn how to bring about their own happiness.

Each one of us is responsible for all of humankind, and for the environment in which we live. We need to think of each other as true brothers and sisters, and need to be deeply concerned with each other's welfare. We must seek to lessen the suffering of others. Rather than working solely to acquire wealth, we need to do something meaningful, something seriously directed toward the welfare of humanity as a whole. To do this, you need to recognize that the whole world is part of you.

Foolish people are always thinking only of themselves, and the result is always negative. Wise people think of others, helping them as much as they can, and the result is happiness. Love and compassion are beneficial, both for you and for others. Through kindness toward others, your mind and heart will open to peace.

Expanding this inner environment to the larger community around you will bring unity, harmony, and cooperation; expanding peace further still to nations, and then to the world, will bring mutual trust, mutual respect, sincere communication, and finally successful joint efforts to solve the world's problems. All this is possible. But the first step is to change ourselves.

Now, let us turn to considering mistakes we commonly make, and how to counteract them. First, let us address the problem of anger, and then the lust that lies behind anger. This leads, in turn, to examining the exaggerations on which these self-defeating emotions are built. I will offer what I hope you will find are helpful techniques, both to alleviate your problems and to develop a kind-hearted outlook that will affect you and those around you in a positive way. If you find these techniques beneficial, please implement them; if not, set them aside for now. They may become helpful later.

I

Does Anger Protect You?

MISTAKE: USING ANGER TO FIGHT ANGER

It may be that if you remain a humble, honest, and contented person, some of your friends, neighbors, coworkers, or rivals will take advantage of you. Simply allowing this to happen may be counterproductive for you, your family, and others. However, anger cannot be overcome by anger. If a person shows anger to you, and you show anger in return, the result is a disaster. If you nurse hatred, you will never be happy, even in the lap of luxury. By contrast, if you control your anger and show its opposite—love, compassion, tolerance, and patience—then not only do you remain in peace, but gradually the anger of others also will diminish.

No one can argue with the fact that in the presence of anger, peace is impossible. It is only through kindness and love that peace of mind can be achieved. Although anger may lead to temporary success, and yield some satisfaction for a brief period, ultimately anger will cause further difficulties. (There is no need to enumerate the many instances of this throughout history, including in this new century.) With anger, all actions are swift. When we face problems with sincere concern for others, success may take longer, but it will be more durable.

When someone is trying to take advantage of you, first you must clearly understand that this other person is a human being, and has a right to be happy. With respect and compassion toward that person, you can act according to the circumstances he or she has created. This means responding strongly if necessary, but never losing your compassionate perspective.

In fact, compassion is the only way to handle such a problem, since anger and irritation will only make effective action more difficult. At first, it may be a struggle to maintain compassion for someone who is being threatening or hurtful, but if you try again and again, you will find the way to react as strongly as the circumstances demand without losing a loving attitude.

Anger needs to be controlled, but not hidden from yourself. Recognize your reactions; do not deny them, for if you do, your compassion will be superficial. When others are mean or nasty to you it is difficult to stay compassionate, but it is not unlike the relationship between kind parents and their children. Sometimes a child is foolish and naughty, and in order to stop that behavior, the mother or father acts in accordance with the circumstances; this may require strong or harsh words, perhaps even punishing the child, but without losing compassion. That is the way to handle the problem.

Summary Reflection

1. If a person shows anger to you, and you show anger in return, the result is a disaster.
2. However, if you control your anger and show its opposite—love, compassion, tolerance, and patience—then not only do you remain in peace, but gradually the anger of others also will diminish.
3. Anger may lead to temporary success, yielding a little satisfaction for a brief period, but ultimately will cause further difficulties.
4. When someone tries to take advantage of you, first you must clearly understand that this person is a human being, and has a right to be happy.
5. Then, you can act according to the circumstances he or she has created, responding strongly if necessary, but never losing your compassionate perspective.

Compassion is the key.

2

Learning That Tough Circumstances Can Be Valuable

MISTAKE: REACTING TO ADVERSE SITUATIONS AS JUST HATEFUL

In my own life, the most difficult periods have been the times when I have gained the most knowledge and experience. If everything is going well, you can maintain the pretense that life is a smooth ride. However, when you face really desperate situations you have to deal with reality. Another benefit of adversity is that hard times can build determination and inner strength. Through them, we can also come to appreciate the uselessness of anger. We can even learn to nurture a deep caring and respect for troublemakers, because, by creating trying circumstances, they provide us with invaluable opportunities to practice tolerance and patience. This is not easy to appreciate, so let us explore this topic further.

During a difficult period you can learn to develop inner

strength, determination, and courage to face your problems. If you become discouraged, that is the real failure; you have lost a valuable chance to develop. To remain determined is itself a gain. During a difficult period you can come closer to reality, to peeling off all pretensions. When things are going smoothly, life can easily become like an official ceremony in which protocol, such as how you walk and how you speak, becomes more important than content. But at a time of crisis it becomes obvious that these ritual trappings are pointless—you have to become more practical.

When we are happy and everything is going according to plan, transformative practice doesn't seem urgent, but when we face unavoidable problems such as sickness, old age, death, or other very difficult situations, it becomes crucial to control our emotions, and to use our good human mind to determine how to face that problem with patience and calm.

My life has not been an altogether happy one; I have had to pass through many difficult times, including losing my country to Chinese Communist invaders, and trying to re-establish our culture in countries outside Tibet. Yet, I regard these difficult periods as among the most important times in my life. Through them, I have gained many new experiences and learned many new ideas.

When I was young and living high above the Tibetan

city of Lhasa in the Potala Palace, I frequently looked at the life of the city through a telescope. I also learned a lot from the gossip of the sweepers in the palace; they served as my newspaper, telling me what the Regent was doing, and what corruption and scandals were going on. I was always happy to listen, and they were proud to be telling the Dalai Lama what was happening in the streets. But the harsh events that unfolded after the invasion in 1950 forced me to become directly involved in issues that otherwise would have been kept at a distance. Over the years, I have come to prefer the life I now lead, committed to social action in this world of suffering.

The most difficult time for me came after the Chinese army invaded Tibet, when I was trying to satisfy the invaders so that the situation would not worsen. When a small delegation of Tibetan officials signed a seventeen-point agreement with the Chinese without my consent, or that of the Tibetan government, we were left with no alternative but to attempt to work within that agreement. Many Tibetans resented it, but when they expressed their opposition, the Chinese reacted even more harshly. I was caught in the middle, trying to cool down the situation.

Without consulting me, the two acting prime ministers of Tibet complained about conditions to the Chinese government; I was then asked to dismiss them. This is the kind of problem I had to face every day, as long as we were in Tibet.

Against Chinese wishes, I went to India in 1956 to celebrate the Buddha's 2,500th birthday. While I was there, I had to make the difficult decision of whether or not to return to Tibet. I was receiving messages about open revolts against the Chinese in eastern Tibet, and many officials in Tibet advised that it would not be safe for me to return. Also, from past experience I knew that as China developed more military strength in Tibet, its attitude would become harsher. We could see that there was not much hope, but at that time it was not clear that we would have a full guarantee of support from the government of India, or from any other government. In the end I chose to return to Tibet, where the situation became more and more complicated and difficult.

Three years later, in 1959, when I joined a mass escape to India, the situation became easier because I no longer faced the dilemma of choosing which path to take. The decision made, we could now put all of our energy and time into building a healthy community, with a modern system of education for our children and young people, while at the same time trying to preserve our traditional ways of studying and practicing Buddhism. Now, we were able to work in an atmosphere of freedom, without fear.

Looking back, I can see how my own practice has benefited from a life of great turbulence and trouble. You, too, can come to see the hardships you endure as deepening your practice.

Real compassion extends to each and every sentient being, not just to friends, or family, or those in terrible situations. True love and compassion extend even to those who wish to harm you. Try to imagine that your enemies are purposefully making trouble in order to help you accumulate positive forces for shaping the future, what Buddhists call "merit," by facing them with patience. If your life goes along too easily, you become soft. Trying circumstances help you develop inner strength, and the courage to face difficulty without emotional breakdown. Who teaches this? Not your friend, but your enemy.

ADVERSITY HELPS
BUILD CHARACTER

Anger destroys love and compassion, and anger is undermined by patience, which is best practiced with an enemy. Without adversaries, you could not fully engage in the practice of patience—tolerance and forbearance. We need enemies to strengthen our practice, and from this spiritual viewpoint we can even be grateful to them. In terms of training in altruism, an enemy is really your guru, your teacher. Since enemies are the greatest teachers of altruism, instead of generating hatred for them, we must view them with gratitude.

Look at it this way: it is not necessary for someone to be favorably disposed toward you in order for you to respect and cherish them. For example, when we want rain and it rains, we are grateful, even though there is no motivation on the part of the shower to help us.

The presence or absence of motivation makes no difference in terms of whether something or someone can help us accumulate merit. Therefore, even though our enemies may be motivated by the desire to harm us, they can do us tremendous good. Enemies are the best way to cultivate the highly meritorious virtue of patience. And without patience, you could not develop true love and compassion, because you would be distracted by irritation.

Meditation

Here is a way to appreciate the value of enemies

1. Consider that in order to build character, the practice of patience is essential.

2. See that the best way to practice patience requires an enemy.
3. Understand that in this way enemies are very valuable for the opportunities they provide.
4. Decide that instead of getting angry with those who block your wishes, you will inwardly respond with gratitude.

By seeing things this way, you can change your attitude toward adversity. This is very difficult, but very rewarding. By considering the matter deeply, you will see that even great enemies who intend you serious harm are also, in a sense, extending great kindness to you. For only when faced with the work of enemies can you learn real inner strength.

Enemies give us this kind of chance. Also, in terms of the practice of patience, an enemy is the most benevolent of helpers. Through cultivating patience your merit increases, therefore enemies are primary instigators of our spiritual advancement.

REFLECTING ON CHANGE

Examine your feelings to see who is being held closely and who is being considered at a distance. Investigate the matter this way:

You naturally feel close to your friend; regarding your enemy, you feel not only distant, but sometimes anger or irritation; you feel nothing for a neutral person. However, it is by no means certain that a friend, an enemy, or a neutral person will at all times either help, harm, or do neither. When you are generating negative thoughts, and negative feelings such as hatred or anger, even a friend is seen as an enemy; when negative thoughts toward an enemy disappear, the enemy becomes a friend.

By reflecting in these ways, you can loosen the hold that afflictive emotions like anger and hatred have on you.

3

Cherishing Others as a Way to Happiness

MISTAKE: BEING EGOTISTICAL

Could you put others first, and consider yourself next? Surprisingly, perhaps, you will find that this approach works even from a selfish viewpoint. Let me explain how this is possible. You want happiness and do not want suffering, and if you show other people kindness, love, and respect, they will respond in kind, increasing your happiness. If you show other people anger and hatred, they will show you the same, and you will lose your own happiness.

So, I say, if you are selfish, be *wisely* selfish. Ordinary selfishness focuses only on your own needs, but if you are wisely selfish, you will treat everyone just as well as you now treat those close to you. This strategy will produce more satisfaction for you, and more happiness. So, even from a selfish viewpoint, you get better results by respecting others, serving others, and reducing your own self-centeredness.

Be wisely selfish. Wise people serve others sincerely, putting the needs of others above their own. The ultimate result will be that you will get more happiness. The kind of selfishness that sets off fighting, quarreling, stealing, and harsh words—forgetting other people's welfare, always thinking "I, I, I,"—will result in your own loss. Others may speak nice words in front of you, but behind your back they will not speak so nicely. They will make note of your selfishness and respond in kind. The remedy is to be sincerely concerned with the well-being of others, and to act accordingly.

After all, even though currently you may not be concerned with other people, you are very much concerned with yourself, no question about it, which means that you must want to achieve a peaceful mind and a happier daily life. The best way to do that is by practicing more kindness and tolerance. There is no need to change the furniture in your house, or move to a new home. Your neighbor may be very noisy, or very difficult, but so long as your own mind is calm and peaceful, neighbors will not bother you much. If you are calm, even your enemy cannot disturb you. However, if you are generally irritable, even when your best friend visits, you cannot become really happy.

This is why I say that you are better off being wisely selfish. This way you can fulfill your selfish motive to be happy. That is much better than being self-centered, or foolishly selfish, which will not succeed in bringing you more happiness.

Try this approach. I think you will be delighted with the result.

4

We Are Our Own Troublemakers

MISTAKE: INFLATING ATTRACTION

Both lust and hatred are based on bias: both develop based on inflating the nature of things far beyond what it actually is. This mistake spawns all other troublesome emotions. Here is how it happens. When you come to the mistaken conclusion that you exist as a fully independent entity (as opposed to being interrelated to other people and things), this leads to an artificial distinction between yourself and others. This, in turn, encourages you to become attached to what you see as being on your own side, and to resist what seems to be on the side of others. This attachment inflates the value of your own qualities, such as physical appearance, ethnic origin, wealth, education, or fame, and opens the door to pride.

So, lust and hatred stem from an exaggerated notion of ourselves as being independent entities, when in fact we depend on many variables, past and present. And once we put too much confidence in a solidly existing, palpable, overly concrete "I," we open the door to discrimination: once there is "I" there is also "you." Discrimination is followed by attachment to our self and anger toward the other, for we get angry at what foils our desires. Anger is fomented by the misconception that its object and you are established as enemy and victim in and of yourselves. And when we get angry, the object of our anger appears far more awful than it truly is. Think about it.

STEPS FROM AWARENESS
TO MISCONCEPTION

Consider the steps by which this happens. When we first encounter something or someone nice, we briefly take notice, acknowledging its presence. The mind at this point is pretty much neutral. But when we pay more attention to it, the object appears to be attractive in a way that is integral to it, instead of having a value that we attached to it. When the mind adheres to an object this way—as if it truly exists the way it appears to—lust for it, and hatred for whatever interferes with getting it can set in. A fundamental mistake about the nature of things has taken hold, and as this illusion of independent existence becomes stronger, the poisons of twisted emotions can take effect.

The turning point from mere awareness to misconception comes when we inflate the goodness or badness of the thing so that it seems *inherently* good or bad, *inherently* attractive or unattractive, *inherently* beautiful or ugly. Accepting this false appearance as fact is an act of ignorance that opens the way for lust, hatred, and myriad other counterproductive emotions. These destructive emotions, in turn, lead to actions based on lust and hatred. These actions, which will eventually lead to suffering, are not seen for what they really are, but are mistaken for a way to happiness.

When our own self is involved, we emphasize this connection: now it is *my* body, *my* stuff, *my* friend, or *my* car. When something we see as desirable is involved, we exaggerate its attractiveness, obscuring its faults and disadvantages, and become excessively attached to it. In this way we are forcibly led into lust, as if by a ring in our nose. When something we see as undesirable is involved, this time we exaggerate the object's unattractiveness, making something minor into a big defect, ignoring other good qualities. We begin to see this object as interfering with our pleasure, and now are being led into hatred, again as if by a ring in our nose.

As you become more self-centered—*my* this, *my* that, *my* body, *my* wealth—anyone who interferes immediately becomes an object of anger. As long as lust, hatred, attachment, jealousy, or confusion are present, all kinds of harmful actions become possible. Under these circumstances every one of us has the potential to do harm, commit a crime, and even commit murder.

Although you make much of *my* friends and *my* relatives, they cannot help you at birth, or at death; you come here alone, and you leave alone. If on the day of your death a friend could accompany you, attachment to that friend might make sense, but this cannot be. When you are reborn into a totally unfamiliar situation, if your friend from the last lifetime could be of some help, that, too, would be something to consider, but this also is not to be. Yet in between birth and death, for many decades, it is *my* friend, *my* sister, *my* brother. This misplaced emphasis does not help at all, except to create more bewilderment and lust. Driven by such lust, you become angry when people do not live up to your expectations. You are not making others happy—and certainly not yourself.

When friends are overemphasized, enemies also come to be overemphasized. When you are born, you do not know anyone, and no one knows you. Even though all of us want happiness and do not want suffering, you like the faces of some people and think, "These are *my* friends," and dislike the faces of others and think, "These are *my* enemies." You affix identities and nicknames to them, and end up practicing the generation of desire for the former and the generation of hatred for the latter. What value is there in this? None.

The problem is that too much energy is being expended on concern for a level no deeper than the superficial affairs of this life. The profound loses out to the trivial. Once you are intent on the fineries of life, your afflictive emotions increase, which, in turn, brings about more bad deeds. These counterproductive actions only lead to trouble, making you and those around you uncomfortable at best. You acquire more and more material things to the point where your practice has become devotion to the superficialities of this life, cultivating desire for friends and hatred for enemies, and trying to figure out ways to act on these afflictive emotions.

WATCH HOW YOU GET INTO TROUBLE

Watch the process by which make a mistake, by imagining a time when you were filled with hatred or lust. Does it not seem that the hated or desired person or thing is extremely substantial, very concrete? But look more closely and you will notice a conflict between appearance and reality. Notice how you:

First perceive the object;

Then determine if the object is good or bad;

Then conclude that the object's goodness or badness exists inherently in the object;

Then generate lust or hatred according to whether the object's goodness or badness has been exaggerated.

The benefit of insight is that it prevents us from attributing goodness or badness beyond what is actually there. This makes it possible to reduce, and perhaps eventually to end, lust and hatred, since these emotions are built on exaggeration. This, in turn, leaves more room for healthy emotions and virtues to develop.

In the next chapter, we will continue this line of investigation.

5

Losing Perspective in Intense Situations

MISTAKE: CONSTRICTING
YOUR OUTLOOK

Lust and hatred narrow our outlook. By focusing on just one particular factor among the many giving rise to a problem, we close the door to broadmindedness. When we see objects as existing in and of themselves, rather than being dependent on many circumstances, as they truly are, exaggeration sets in: If the object seems favorable, we become attached to it, thinking, "This is really wonderful." Once desire increases, anger will arise against whoever or whatever might interfere with our enjoyment. The problem is that both lust and hatred are based on bias, which makes true compassion impossible.

We lust after pleasurable forms, sounds, odors, tastes, and touches, and anger arises when this lust is thwarted, whether due to an interfering person or to some outside circumstance. When we lose our temper in such cases, we have no hesitation about speaking harsh words, even to a close friend. But afterwards, when we cool down, we feel embarrassed about what happened. This indicates that fundamentally we do not want to use harsh words, but because we allowed our perspective to be distorted by anger, we lost control of ourselves.

One day my driver in Tibet was working under my car and bumped his head against the chassis; he got so angry, he hit his head against the car a couple of times to punish the vehicle, but, of course, he only hurt himself.

When we do not challenge appearances, but assent to them, and consider an object or person to be good or bad through and through, this causes us to desire it unduly, or to feel unwarranted hatred for it. At such times we make strong statements, like "He is awful!" "She is really terrible!" "This cake is terrific!" "That restaurant is fantastic!" At the point when anger and lust are generated, reality has become obscured; instead, we see extreme badness or extreme goodness, evoking twisted, unrealistic actions.

Let me tell you a story. When my Senior Tutor, Ling Rinpoche, was still in Tibet before the Chinese invasion, he wanted a table lacquered, so he asked his attendant to take it to a Chinese artisan who was living in Lhasa. When his attendant arrived at the shop, the artisan was sitting with a broken antique teacup in his hand, staring at it and sighing. He told the attendant that earlier he had gotten angry and banged the cup down, shattering it. He had been viewing a customer in his shop as one hundred percent horrible and broke the cup to satisfy his rage. Now that his anger had subsided, he again saw the cup as a beautiful antique, and so he was holding it in his hand, sighing with regret. His warped perspective had melted away.

In situations like this, you can clearly see that lust and hatred are based on going along with the appearance of qualities, such as goodness or badness, as if they truly, objectively exist in those persons or objects. This does not mean that good and bad, or favorable and unfavorable, do not exist, for they do, but it means that these qualities do not exist independently in the way that they appear to a lustful or a hateful mind.

Even if an object—an event, a person, or any other phenomenon—has a slightly favorable aspect, once the object is mistakenly seen as existing totally from its own side, independently of other circumstances, mental projection has exaggerated its goodness beyond what it actually is, triggering lust. The same is true of anger and hatred; this time a negative factor is being exaggerated, making the object seem a hundred percent negative, without any mitigating qualities. The result is deep disturbance. An experienced psychotherapist told me that when we generate anger, ninety percent of the ugliness of the object of our anger is due to our own exaggeration. This is very much in conformity with the Buddhist idea of how afflictive emotions arise.

INTERDEPENDENCE

All of this can be avoided by seeing the fuller picture, which is revealed by paying attention to the dependent nature of phenomena, the nexus of causes and conditions from which they arise, and in which they exist. Once we see things as interconnected and therefore interdependent, the mistaken view that leads to afflictive emotions becomes obvious. If you want to be able to perceive the actual situation, you have to quit submitting voluntarily to these destructive emotions, because, in each and every field, they obstruct the truth. Viewed from the perspective of lust or anger, for example, the facts are always obscured. Lust and hatred are simply unrealistic.

Under the influence of these warped emotions, your outlook is necessarily constricted, limited to its target. For example, when you become angry at a painful situation, you do not see the web of conditions that contribute to it, whereas if you saw the full extent of those contributing factors, hatred would be impossible.

Afflictive emotions require a fixed target, seemingly real and autonomous. When these destructive emotions take the stage, it becomes all the harder to see that the situation is dependent on a multitude of interrelated circumstances, and thereby harder to figure out how to change the situation. In the absence of lust and hatred, however, this web of interrelatedness is much easier to see.

To overcome the misconception that things and people exist as self-sufficient entities, independent of the way we perceive them, it is essential to observe your own mind to discover how this mistake is being conceived, and how other destructive emotions arise supported by such ignorance. Given that lust, hatred, pride, jealousy, and anger stem from exaggerating the importance of such qualities as beauty and ugliness, it is crucial to understand how things actually exist, without exaggeration. When you begin to see that this assignment of extreme virtue or evil to a person or object is what makes them an object of lust or hatred, the emotion built on that exaggeration backs off; we see the mistake we have made, and we pull back.

Putting an end to our troubles rests on understanding interdependence, which Buddhists call "dependent-arising." The mistaken perception that people and things exist in and of themselves gives rise to mistaken thinking, which in turn generates the harmful emotions of lust and hatred, a cycle that goes on and on almost without end. Those destructive emotions produce actions infected by them, and these actions leave imprints in the mind that drive repeated cycles of pain. We can put an end to this process by cultivating our own awareness of dependence, reliance, and interconnectivity.

Consider How Phenomena Appear in an Intense Situation

1. Remember a time when you felt intense hatred or lust. The hated or desired person or thing seemed extremely substantial, didn't it?
2. When you reflect on how things appeared to you in such an intense situation, you will find that they seemed to exist in their own right.
3. However, the fact is that nothing exists in this way; everything is set up in dependence on its causes, its parts, and on the way we perceive it.
4. When you notice your own exaggerated reactions, you will see that you have lost sight of the fact that people and things are dependent on an interrelated web of factors and conditions.

5. Keep trying to see and feel how your focus narrows in intense situations of lust and anger. When you notice this confinement, you will naturally want to loosen the bonds of the exaggerated emotions that keep you there.

From the day we are born, we undergo many calamities. If there is a way of eliminating, or at least diminishing, these obstacles to our happiness, surely we should consider it.

6

Being Ready for Change

MISTAKE: THINKING YOU
WILL ALWAYS BE HERE

One of the chief reasons why lust and hatred arise is that we are overly attached to the current flow of life. We have a sense that it will last forever, and with that sort of attitude, we become fixated on superficialities—material possessions, and temporary friends and situations. To overcome this foolishness you need to reflect on the fact that a day is coming when you will not be here.

No matter how long we live, at most around one hundred years, eventually we must die, losing this valuable human life. And this could happen at any time. No matter how much prosperity we enjoy, this life will disintegrate. No amount of wealth can buy us an extension. On the day of your death, nothing you have accumulated can help; we have to leave it all behind. In this respect, the death of a rich person and the death of a wild animal are alike.

Even though there is no certainty that you will die

tonight, when you cultivate an awareness of death, you appreciate that you *could* die tonight. With this attitude, if there is something you can do that will help both in the present and the future, you will give it precedence over something that will help in just a superficial way. Furthermore, by being uncertain about when death will come, you will refrain from doing something that will harm both your present and your future. You will be motivated to develop outlooks that act as antidotes to the various forms of untamed mind. Then, whether you live a day, a week, a month, or a year, that time will be meaningful, because your thoughts and actions will be based on what is beneficial in the long run. By contrast, when you come under the influence of the illusion of permanence and spend your time on matters that go no deeper than the surface of this life, you sustain great loss.

MATERIAL CONTENTMENT

It is better right from the beginning to be content with our material situation, which is limited by its very nature. However, since there is no limit to compassion and altruism, we should not be content with the degree that we have achieved. Unfortunately, we often feel just the opposite: spiritually, we are content with slight amounts of practice and progress, but, materially, we always want more and more. It should be the other way around. It is a mistake to think that just because you have more money it is worthwhile to spend more on food, clothing, and adornments for yourself. Instead, spend more on health and education for poor people. This is not forced socialism, but voluntary compassion.

Contentment is the key. If you are content with regard to material things, you are truly rich. Without contentment, even if you are a billionaire, you will not have happiness. You will always feel hungry for more and more and more, making you not rich, but poor. If you seek contentment externally, it will never come. Your desire will never be fulfilled.

Our Tibetan Buddhist texts tell of a king who gained control over the world, at which point he began thinking about taking over the lands of the gods. In the end, his good qualities were destroyed by his inability to find fulfillment, and by his pride.

Contentment is necessary for happiness, so try to be satisfied with adequate food, clothing, and shelter. For a layperson, sexual excitement is generally not considered to be wrong, but too much emphasis on it can bring disaster. Everything needs to be felt and acted upon in a balanced way. This is essential. Too much excitement and sexual attachment can sow the seeds of divorce.

It is crucial to be mindful of impermanence—to contemplate that you will not remain long in this life. If you are not aware of death, you will fail to take advantage of this special human life that you have already attained. Contemplation of the imminence of death brings more energy to life, and if you accept that death is part of life, then when it actually does come, you will face it more easily. When people know deep inside that death will come but deliberately avoid thinking about it, that is counterproductive. The same is true when old age is not accepted as part of life but is seen as undesirable, and therefore deliberately avoided as a consideration. This leads to being mentally unprepared; then, when old age inevitably occurs, it is very difficult.

The best way to overcome counterproductive attachments is to realize that it is the nature of life that what has gathered will eventually disperse—parents, children, brothers, sisters, and friends. No matter how much people love each other, eventually they must part. The mistake is to see these situations as permanent. Attachment is built on this misperception, and will always cause more pain.

Turning away from attachment does not mean that

you should ignore essential needs, such as food, shelter, and sleep. Rather, you should separate yourself from superficial distractions that elicit such exclamations as, "This is wonderful!" "I must have this!" "Oh, if I only could have this!" When you give your life over to such thoughts, finery and money become more attractive than spiritual development; distressing emotions increase, leading to trouble, disturbing yourself and those around you, while you figure out ways to satisfy these emotions, causing yet more trouble. Run ragged by attachment, you find no comfort.

Under the sway of attachment, the object of our desires appears to be good through and through, but, in reality, it is not that way. When attachment starts to develop, try to find negative qualities in the object of your desire. Once attachment has set in, it is very difficult to suppress; at that point your best chance is to try distracting your attention from the object, perhaps even physically leaving it behind.

An outlook based on permanence is ruinous. When the present becomes your preoccupation, the future does not matter, which undermines your motivation to engage in compassionate practices for the sake of others. Good fortune is not permanent, so it is dangerous to become too attached to things going well. An outlook of impermanence helps. By seeing that the true nature of things is transitory, you will not be shocked by change when it occurs, not even the change brought about by aging and death.

Compared to the lifespan of this planet, the maximum duration of a human life is very short. This brief existence should be used in such a way that it does not create pain for others. It should be committed to more constructive activities—at least to not harming others, or creating trouble for them. In this way, our brief span on this planet will be meaningful. If a tourist visits a certain place for a short period and creates trouble, that is silly. But if, as a tourist you make others happy during this short period, that is wise; when you yourself move on to your next place, you feel happy. If you create problems, even though you yourself do not encounter any difficulty during your stay, you will wonder: what was the use of my visit?

Accepting old age and death as part of life is crucial to making life meaningful. Feeling that death is remote or impossible leads to greediness and more trouble—sometimes even to doing deliberate harm to others. When we take a good look at how supposedly great people—emperors, monarchs, and so forth—built huge dwelling places and walls, we see that deep inside their minds was an idea that they would stay in this life forever to enjoy these things. This self-deception results in more pain for many people.

Even for those who do not believe in future lifetimes, contemplation of the reality of impermanence is productive, helpful, and even scientific. Because people, minds, and all other phenomena change moment by moment, it opens up the possibility for positive development. If situations did not change, they would forever retain the nature of suffering. Once you understand that things are always changing, even if you are going through a very difficult period, you can find comfort in knowing that the situation will not remain that way forever. There is no need for frustration.

BEING AWARE THAT YOU COULD DIE AT ANY TIME WILL HELP TO DEFLATE ATTACHMENT

If you do not wait until the end for the knowledge that you will die to sink in, if you realistically assess your situation now, you will not be overwhelmed by superficial, temporary goals. You will not neglect what matters in the long run. It is better to decide from the very beginning that you will die, and then investigate what is worthwhile. If you keep in mind how quickly this life disappears, you will value your time and do what is most valuable. With a strong sense of the imminence of death, you will feel the need to engage in spiritual practice, improving your mind instead of wasting your time on various distractions, ranging from eating and drinking to endless talk about sports, war, romance, and gossip. Try to keep in mind this famous Indian saying, "A tomorrow when you are gone is undoubtedly coming."

If our human body were stable and permanent—not prone to deterioration—we could put off until later making the best of it. However, life is fragile and easily damaged by any number of external and internal causes. Since the body depends on so many factors that work in opposition to each other, physical happiness is just the occasional balance of these elements, not an enduring harmony. For instance, if you are cold, at first heat feels good, but too much starts to feel unpleasant. The same is true of disease; medicine for one ailment may bring on another malady, which then has to be counteracted. Physical comfort is merely the temporary absence of such problems and complications.

Our bodies must be sustained by food, but when you eat too much, the very thing needed to create health becomes a source of sickness and pain. In countries where food is scarce, hunger and starvation cause great suffering, but in those countries where nutritious food is plentiful, there is still suffering, this time from overeating and indigestion. When there is balance, without any manifest problems, we call this "happiness," but it would be foolish to think that we had become, or could ever become, free from disease or suffering. It is not as if in the absence of disease, or war, or starvation, we would not die. It is the nature of things to disintegrate. Right from conception, the body is subject to the forces that lead to death.

VALUING YOUR LIFE

So, this human life is a precious endowment, potent yet fragile. Simply by virtue of being alive, you are at a very important juncture, and carry a great responsibility. You can achieve powerful good for yourself and others, so becoming distracted by the minor affairs of this lifetime would be a tremendous waste. Resolve to use this lifetime in this body effectively, urging yourself on from the inside and seeking whatever assistance there is from the outside. You should use your fleeting life for your benefit and that of others. Physical happiness is just an occasional balance of elements in the body, not a deep harmony. Recognize the temporary for what it is. Do not assume that there will be time later.

Meditative Reflection

1. It is certain that I will die. Death cannot be avoided. My lifetime is running out and cannot be extended.

2. When I will die is unknown. Human lifespan varies. The causes of death are many, and the causes of life comparatively few. The body is fragile.

3. We are all in this same tenuous situation, so there is no point in quarrelling and fighting, or wasting all our mental and physical energy on accumulating money and property.

4. By mistaking what deteriorates moment by moment for something constant, I bring pain upon myself as well as others. I should reduce my attachment to passing fancies.

5. From the depths of my heart, I should seek to get beyond these cycles of suffering created by mistaking what is fleeting for permanent.

6. In the long run, what helps most is my transformed attitude.

Being aware of impermanence calls for discipline—taming the mind—but this does not mean punishment, or control from the outside. Discipline does not mean prohibition; rather, it means that when there is a contradiction between short-term and long-term interests, you sacrifice the former for the latter. This is *self*-discipline, which is based on understanding the cause and effect of one's own actions. This type of discipline offers protection. A tamed mind makes you peaceful, relaxed, and happy, whereas if your mind is not disciplined in this way, no matter how wonderful your external circumstances, you will be beset by fears and worries. Realize that the root of your own happiness and welfare lies in a peaceful and tamed mind. It is also a great benefit to those around you.

Human beings have all the potential necessary to create good things, but its full utilization requires freedom. Totalitarianism stifles this growth. Individualism means that you do not expect something from the outside, or that you are waiting for orders; rather, you yourself create the initiative. Therefore, Buddha frequently called for "individual liberation," meaning self-liberation, rather than freedom achieved through large-scale political or military action. Each individual must create his or her own positive future. Freedom and individualism require self-discipline. If they are exploited by afflictive emotions, there will be negative consequences. Freedom and self-discipline must work together.

7

Is Anger Useful?

MISTAKE: IMAGINING THAT ANGER HELPS

There are two classes of emotions. One class needs to be expressed, and talked about. Take depression, for example. Perhaps someone close to you has died, and you are grieving privately. If, instead of hiding your feelings, you express them openly to a friend, the overwhelming power of that sadness will become more bearable. The other class of emotions includes anger, strong attachment, and strong lust; these do not diminish when they are expressed. On the contrary.

For instance, if anger is expressed today, tomorrow there may be more, whereas if you try to minimize your anger, it will weaken. We can see this in our own experience. Giving anger the weapons of words and actions is like giving an unruly child a pile of straw and a box of matches. Once lit, anger feeds off the air of exposure and can rage quickly out of control. The only alternative is to control anger, and the way to do this is to think, "What is the value of anger? How does that compare to the value of tolerance and compassion?"

When those who do not consider the disadvantages of afflictive emotions, such as anger, are distressed and get riled up, they feel they are perfectly right, even if they have a tiny bit of concern about how people might view them. Since they consider getting riled up to be normal, they make no effort to reduce anger.

On the other hand, those who consider afflictive emotions to be negative and harmful do not welcome anger. Sometimes anger might win out and control them, but deep inside they are resisting its effects. Even if they do not take sufficient countermeasures, their inner reluctance about getting angry makes a great difference in the long run. This is why it is important to reflect on the drawbacks of anger.

Use your common sense. Is anger useful? If you get angry with someone, is the result good for you or for the other person? Nothing helpful comes of it. And, in the end, anger harms you more than anyone else. When you are angry, good food is not tasty. When you are angry, even the faces of your spouse, children, or friends are irritating, not because their faces have changed but because something is wrong with your own attitude.

On the other hand, when an unfortunate event occurs,

you can handle it more effectively in the absence of anger. Anger is almost useless. A harsh word may be spoken sometimes to keep someone from doing something stupid, but anger should not be its primary motive; love and compassion should be. Actions stemming solely from anger are of no use at all; realizing this can strengthen your determination to resist them.

Remember, anger is a turbulent state of mind based on exaggeration that makes something (another person, your own pain, or even a cause of pain like a thorn) seem more unpleasant than it really is; hatred rages against that object and drives us to do it harm. When you get angry, you create additional discomfort for yourself and among those around you. Even bystanders feel awkward, and intimates are saddened and disturbed. If hateful actions are taken, the disturbance spreads further. In this way, destructive emotions ruin your life and the lives of others in your family and community. All the many upsets that are so prevalent in the world stem from the three disturbances of lust, hatred, and ignorance.

Reflection on the Problems with Anger

Here is how to reflect meditatively on the disadvantages of anger:

1. *Anger creates havoc*

   Anger motivates rude words and harsh physical actions, immediately creating an unpleasant atmosphere. Anger diminishes your power to distinguish right from wrong, an ability that is one of the highest human attributes. When it is lost, we are lost. Sometimes it is necessary to respond strongly, but this can be done without anger. Anger is not necessary. It has no value.

2. *Anger magnifies problems*

   Even small actions can lead to huge effects, just as a small seed can give rise to a great tree. For instance, uttering an ugly name to describe another person while motivated by anger can have rippling effects far into the future.

3. *Anger undermines virtues*

   The ability of a virtuous deed to generate a good effect can be undermined by strong anger, which makes it doubly important to control your rage. If, after you performed a virtuous action and accumulated its potential, the potential benefit of that good deed remained intact without diminishing until its positive fruit issued forth, the situation would not be so tenuous, but that is not the case. Instead, the effect of a strong, nonvirtuous state of mind, such as anger, overpowers the potential future benefit of a virtuous act so that it cannot issue forth, much like scorching a seed.

Conversely, a strong virtuous attitude overpowers the negative potential established by misdeeds, making them unable to issue their effects. Therefore it is necessary not only to take many actions that will set in motion future good effects, but also to avoid setting in motion negative forces that would undercut the future benefit of the good you are doing.

As you analyze this situation more and more, gradually your convictions about the uselessness of anger will strengthen. Repeated reflection on the disadvantages of anger will cause you to realize that it is senseless, even pathetic. When it becomes obvious that the effects of anger are harmful, you will arrive at the conclusion that there are no positive results to be found in anger, hatred, and violence. This decision will cause you to be less and less willing to acquiesce to negativity.

MAINTAIN INTROSPECTION

At those times when your senses encounter pleasant or unpleasant objects, practice keeping your mind from falling into lust or hatred by recognizing their disadvantages; be determined not to sanction them. Then, mindful that these emotions need to be restrained, you can become more attentive to situations that might generate self-destructive emotions. When such situations occur, see if afflictive emotions are being generated. You need to maintain this vigilance no matter what you are doing. In this way, you can make use of each day of your life, while recognizing that lust and hatred continue to arise from time to time.

EXAMINE THESE SEEMINGLY SOLID APPEARANCES

You are getting angry because someone has harmed, is harming, or will harm you, your family, or your friend. In that flash of rage you feel that both the subject (I), and the object (the enemy), are tangible, independent entities. Because you mistakenly accept the appearance of things, anger is generated. However, there is an alternative. At, or even before, that first flash of rage, use reason to examine:

Who am I?
Who is this one who is being hurt?
What is the enemy?
Is the enemy the body of this other person?
Is the enemy his or her mind?

If you examine things in this way, the enemy who previously seemed to be created in and of herself or himself as something to get angry at, and this "I" who was inherently created to be hurt, seem to disappear. And the anger breaks apart.

Do not expect immediate results from practicing this way, or you may become discouraged. Usually my advice for beginners is to be patient; have few expectations of yourself. It is most important to be an honest member of the human community. Whether or not you understand profound ideas, it is important to be a good person wherever you are right now. Consider both the present and the long term in the same way that temporary economic gains should be considered in relation to long-term needs. Do not neglect a greater purpose for the sake of a smaller one. Through such ongoing, thoughtful contemplation, your affinity for hatred will diminish, and your esteem for compassion will increase. Irritation will gradually change its color. All good qualities have to be sown and cultivated over months and years. You cannot expect to go to sleep tonight as an ordinary person and rise tomorrow having attained high spiritual realization.

8

The Conflict Between Appearance and Reality

MISTAKE: TAKING THE SURFACE AS ALL THERE IS

As I have been saying, ignorance leads to exaggerating the importance of beauty, ugliness, and other qualities, which leads to lust, hatred, jealousy, and belligerence. Understand that these are mistaken attitudes, and that their root—the ignorant conception that phenomena exist in their own right—is also mistaken. It has no valid foundation. Work at generating the wisdom that realizes that everything is interdependent, or relative.

As you cultivate this insight more and more, it will naturally become stronger and stronger, and you will find yourself less and less susceptible to counterproductive emotions. Now, you allow yourself to notice the deeper continuum of life that usually goes unnoticed, and to cultivate true concern for others. You gradually refuse to voluntarily rush into what are actually superficial responses to exaggerated appearances, and, instead, you take time to probe what lies beneath the surface.

When encountering various good and bad objects, you should not be attached to their appearance, but see them as like illusions; this will keep you from coming under the influence of harmful emotions like lust or anger. Let me explain.

There are many discrepancies between the way things appear and the way they really are. Something that is impermanent can appear to be permanent. Also, sources of pain, such as overeating, sometimes first appear to be sources of pleasure, but, in the end, they are not. They actually bring us trouble. Although we want happiness, in our ignorance we do not know how to achieve it; although we do not want pain, we misunderstand its workings, so we end up contributing to its causes.

In Buddhist texts, magical displays, reflections, and mirages are used to provide a rough idea of the conflict between what something appears to be and what it actually is. It is not that you and others *are* illusions; rather, you are *like* illusions, which, although they appear to exist in and of themselves, do not. As Buddha said, "All things have the attribute of falsity, deceptiveness."

The eyes of those attending a magic show are affected by the magician's tricks, and, due to this deception, the audience thinks it sees horses, elephants, an appetizing meal, or an attractive woman or man. In a similar way, by going along with the appearance of things we exaggerate the status of good and bad phenomena, and are thereby led into lust and hatred; these then give rise to counterproductive actions that leave negative imprints, called karmas, in our minds. What does not exist in and of itself appears to exist that way, and we accept it as such; by doing so we are led into trouble. For instance, while we are very angry with someone, we have a strong sense of their wretchedness, but later, when we calm down and look at that same person, we may find our earlier perceptions and actions regrettable, even laughable.

Meditation

To avoid being mired in appearances, try viewing phenomena as being like illusions in this way:

1. The reflection of a face is undeniably produced in dependence on a face and a mirror, and is empty of the eyes, ears, and other features it appears to have.
2. The reflection of a face undeniably disappears when either face or mirror is absent.
3. Similarly, even though a person does not have

even a speck of independent existence, it is not contradictory for a person to perform actions and to experience the effects of those actions.

Because lust and hatred stem from our accepting the appearance of inflated qualities—good or bad—the practice of seeing people and things as being like an illusion, like a show with a false facade, helps reduce unfavorable emotions.

Now, you can leave room for developing positive qualities, like compassion, which are built on seeing things as they really are, not on ignorant exaggeration.

9

The Malleable Nature
of the Mind

MISTAKE: VIEWING LUST
AND HATRED AS INTEGRAL
TO THE MIND

Counterproductive emotions such as lust, hatred, and jealousy all depend upon the initial mistake that you, others, and all things exist as independent entities, whereas actually they do not. In our ignorance, we accept that things exist in and of themselves, generating all these distressing emotions that we suffer day by day.

It may seem that emotions like lust, hatred, and jealousy are so integral to the workings of our mind that they are unavoidable. However, when we analyze whether these attitudes are intrinsic to the nature of the mind itself, we find that, as the great Indian scholar-yogi Dharmakirti said, "The nature of the mind is clear light; defilements are superficial." The nature of our innermost subtle consciousness is pure; anger, attachment, and so forth are peripheral to the basic mind.

We call this basic consciousness the *fundamental, inborn mind of clear light*. Because it makes transformation possible, it is also called our *inner nature of enlightenment*. It exists at the root of all consciousness. This means that you are already equipped with the basic quality needed to attain complete enlightenment—the luminous and cognitive nature of your own mind. Also, all of us already have some level of compassion, despite differences in its development and scope, and all of us have an intelligence that distinguishes between favorable and unfavorable. Because these conditions can be developed to a greater and greater degree, they are the foundations of transformation.

There is no external means for removing destructive emotions. If a thorn pierces you, you can remove it forever with a needle, but, to get rid of an unfavorable attitude, you must see clearly the mistaken beliefs on which is it based. Once we learn that these counterproductive attitudes do not dwell in the basic nature of the mind, we can remove them by generating antidotes to them, perspectives that, like medicine, can counteract them.

If warped outlooks were inseparable from our basic mind, then, as long as our mind functioned, ruinous thoughts and feelings such as anger would have to exist, but this is not the case. Obviously not. Right at the moment when you sneeze, for example, you cannot be angry. If distressing emotions such as anger were basic to the mind, then the mind would always have to be angry. Only under certain circumstances do we become irate; when those conditions are not present, neither is our anger. At this very instant your mind is reading and thinking, so anger is probably not present. Attitudes such as anger and attachment can be separated from the main mind.

At times in our lives, our minds hold on to anger and attachment, and at other times our minds manifest detachment, contentment, love, and compassion. We cannot feel desire and hatred toward the very same object at exactly the same time. We can certainly have these feelings at different times, and even sometimes in rapid succession, but not in the very same moment, which shows that these two attitudes cannot coexist. They oppose each other: when one of them increases in strength, the other decreases.

AFFLICTIVE EMOTIONS ARE BASED ON A MISTAKE

Impure states of mind such as desire and hatred are not part of the basic nature of the mind, and must be produced with the assistance of ignorance. All faulty states of mind are mistaken at their root. Ignorance is a form of consciousness mistaken with respect to the object of its attention; it is wrong about it. But valid consciousnesses— the opposites of lust and hatred—operate even when there is no mistaken belief in independent existence.

Valid cognition supports love and compassion, for instance. These positive qualities need no assistance from the ignorance that misconceives objects as existing in and of themselves alone, whereas nonvirtuous attitudes, such as hatred, pride, and so forth, are generated *only* with the assistance and support of ignorance. Without this misunderstanding of the nature of things, there is no way that lust and hatred can operate.

Sensible desires draw favorable things to us, but lust fails at this task because at its core it is biased and therefore clouded. With lust what seems to be affection for another is prejudiced, so that even the slightest interference allows hatred to set in. Altruism, on the other hand, is supremely effective at drawing beneficial factors together, because its unbiased nature will never spur us to do irrational harm.

Similarly, although hatred is mistaken to be integral to the mind, it is not; it is an attitude without valid support. Compassion, however, is founded in truth. When, over a long period of time, an attitude that has a valid foundation competes with an attitude that does not, the one with the valid foundation will overwhelm the other. This is why when you become accustomed to correct attitudes through practice, faulty states of mind naturally diminish, until finally they are extinguished.

WATCHING THE MIND'S LUMINOUS NATURE

To do this, you need to develop an ability to watch your thoughts. As long as all of your consciousness is steeped in conceptual thinking, it is difficult for thought to observe thought. If, however, when thoughts arise, you are able to split off a mental observer that watches them, gradually you will develop a faculty of consciousness observing consciousness; now, even at moments of hatred, a factor from within your mind will be able to step outside the anger. By becoming familiar with consciousness as both knower and object known, you can come to recognize what is called "ordinary mind," which is unaffected by liking and not liking, wanting and not wanting.

Consciousness is luminous in the double sense that its nature is clear and that it illuminates, or reveals, like a lamp that dispels darkness so that objects may be seen. The luminous nature of the mind is not diminished even by afflictive emotions like hatred. Just as the basic nature of water is not polluted by filth, no matter how dirty, the inner nature of even a troubled mind is not defiled by those negative emotions. When the mind is not fractured into many different functions, its natural state of luminous knowing can be recognized, and if you stay with it, the experience of luminosity and knowing will increase. When this happens, hatred will gradually melt into the nature of consciousness.

UNDERMINING AFFLICTIVE EMOTIONS BY KNOWING THEIR NATURE

Learn to separate a corner of the mind from strong emotions, and observe them; this will show you that the mind and attitudes like hatred are not one. Then you will know from experience that when you get irritated, you can concentrate on the underlying nature of the anger and thereby undermine its force.

External circumstance is not what draws us into suffering. Suffering is caused and permitted by an untamed mind. The appearance of self-defeating emotions in our minds leads us into faulty actions. The naturally pure mind is covered over by these emotions and troubling thoughts, which push us into faulty actions, inevitably leading to suffering. We need, with great awareness and care, to extinguish these problematic attitudes, the way gathering clouds dissolve back into the sky.

When our self-defeating attitudes, emotions, and conceptions cease, so will the harmful actions arising from them. As the great late-eleventh-century and early-twelfth-century Tibetan yogi Milarepa said, "When arising, arising within space itself; when dissolving, dissolving back into space." We need to become familiar with the state of our own minds to understand how to dissolve ill-founded ideas and impulses in the deeper sphere of reality. The sky was there before the clouds gathered, and it will be there after they have gone. It is also present when the clouds seem to cover every inch of the sky we can see.

As we've seen, the basic nature of water is not polluted by filth, and in the same way, the mind of clear light remains pure. The next time you feel hatred, see if you can split off an observer from the main run of your mind to watch the hatred. Whereas, we usually feel, "I hate . . . ," as if our sense of self and hatred are totally bound up with each other, here you are watching hatred from a slight distance, seeing its faults, which itself naturally causes this excited state to settle down.

You do not have to stop the various thoughts and feelings that dawn to the mind; just do not get caught up in them, do not let your mind be drawn into them. The mind will then take its own natural form, and the basic purity of its clear light can emerge and be known.

MEDITATION

It is very helpful each day to identify the nature of the mind and concentrate on it. However, it is difficult to catch hold of the mind, hidden as it is beneath our own scattered thoughts. As a technique to identify the basic nature of the mind:

1. First stop remembering what happened in the past.
2. Then stop thinking about what might happen in the future.
3. Let the mind flow of its own accord without the overlay of thought. Observe it for a while in its natural state.

When, for instance, you hear a noise, between the time you hear it and the time you identify its source you can sense a state of mind devoid of thought but not asleep, in which you experience the sound as a reflection of the mind's luminosity and knowing. At such a time you can grasp the basic nature of the mind. In the beginning, when you are not used to this practice, it is quite difficult, but, in time, the mind appears like clear water. Try to stay with this state of mind without being distracted by thoughts, and become accustomed to it.

Practice this meditation in the early morning, when your mind has awakened and is clear, but your senses are not yet fully operating. It helps not to have eaten too much the night before; the quality of your sleep will be lighter, which makes the mind lighter and sharper the next morning. If you eat too much, your sleep can be thick and heavy, such that you are almost like a corpse. In my own daily routine, I eat my fill at breakfast and lunch, but just a little bit at night—less than half a cup of crackers; then I go to bed early and rise at three-thirty in the morning to begin meditation.

See if paying attention to the nature of the mind early in the morning makes your mind more alert throughout the day. Your thoughts certainly will be more tranquil. Also, your memory will improve if you are able to practice a little meditation every day, withdrawing from the scattered mind. This conceptual mind that runs on thinking of good things, bad things, and so forth will get a rest. A little nonconceptuality can provide a much-needed vacation.

Regardless of the nature of the world, you will not suffer affliction or cause suffering when you trust in the mind's fundamental nature of luminosity, its clear light. When the mind knows its own nature, and when this knowledge is teamed with powerful concentration, gradually it becomes possible to reduce and, finally, to overcome the afflictive states that drive the process of repeated suffering.

It is crucial to realize that counterproductive emotions such as spite, jealousy, and belligerence do not reside in the very essence of mind, but are peripheral to it. Even while generating a great many states like lust, hatred, and bewilderment, the basic nature of the mind itself is free from the corruption of these attitudes. Like the clear sky that lies behind the clouds, its nature always remains clear.

No matter what afflictive emotions are generated, and no matter how powerful they are, the basic mind itself remains unaffected; it is good without beginning or end. Wonderful spiritual qualities, such as unbounded love and compassion, are all present in basic form in this diamond mind; their manifestation is prevented only by certain temporary conditions. In a sense, we are enlightened from the very beginning, endowed with a completely good basic mind.

10

Compassion, the Root of Relationships

Whenever I speak with people, I do so with the sense that I am a member of their family. Although you and I may be meeting for the first time, I accept you as a friend. I do so not as a Buddhist, nor as a Tibetan, nor as the Dalai Lama. I do so as one human being speaking with another.

I hope that at this moment you are thinking of yourself as a human being rather than as an American, Asian, European, African, or member of any particular country. These loyalties are secondary. If you and I find common ground as human beings, we can communicate on a basic level. If I think, "I am a monk," or "I am a Buddhist," these are peripheral in comparison to my nature as a human being.

To be human is basic, the foundation from which we all arise. You are born as a human being and that cannot change until you die. Everything else—whether you are educated or uneducated, young or old, rich or poor—is secondary. In truth, you and I already know each other, profoundly, as human beings who share the same basic goals. We all seek happiness, and we do not want suffering.

In big cities, on farms, in remote places, throughout the countryside, people are moving busily. Why? We are all motivated by the desire to make ourselves happy. To do so is right. However, we must keep in mind that too much involvement in the superficial aspects of life will not solve our larger problem of discontentment. Love, compassion, and concern for others are the real sources of happiness. With these in abundance, you will not be disturbed by even the most uncomfortable circumstances. If you nurse hatred, however, you will not be happy even in the midst of wealth. So, if we really want happiness, we must widen the sphere of love. This is both religious thinking and basic common sense.

We are all born helpless. Without a parent's kindness we could not survive, much less prosper. When children grow up in constant fear, with no one to rely on, they suffer their whole lives. Because the minds of small children are very delicate, their need for kindness is particularly obvious, but adults need kindness, too.

If someone greets me with a nice smile, and expresses a genuinely friendly attitude, I appreciate it very much. Though I might not know that person, or even understand their language, my heart is instantly gladdened. On the other hand, if kindness is lacking, even in someone from my own culture whom I have known for many years, I feel it. Kindness and love, a real sense of sisterhood and brotherhood, these are very precious. They make community possible, and therefore are an essential part of any society.

As small children, we depend on the kindness of our parents. In old age, again we depend on the kindness of others. Between childhood and old age we falsely believe we are independent, but this is not so.

Human society exists because it is impossible to live in complete isolation. We are interdependent by nature, and since we must live together, we should do so with a positive attitude of concern for one another. The aim of society must be the compassionate betterment of all from one lifetime to the next—not just humans, but all beings living on this planet. When you gain more appreciation both for the kindness intentionally bestowed on you by others and for the unintended kindnesses reflected in the goods and services you depend on daily, you will contribute to a healthier society. Without appreciation of kindness, society breaks down.

While many in this world are enjoying increasing prosperity, many also remain in extreme poverty. In most countries there is a vast disparity between social classes. Everywhere, the poor are terribly vulnerable. It is particularly saddening nowadays to realize that many people in dire distress are not being helped due to political considerations. Some suffer indirectly from governments allocating too much money for weapons and armies, while neglecting basic needs, such as agriculture. As a result, when a natural disaster hits, the situation is hopeless. Others suffer directly, as we see when there is government-sanctioned discrimination against a particular community.

That people in need are ignored, abandoned, or exploited for political reasons reveals what we are lacking: although we are intelligent and powerful enough to destroy the world, we lack real kindness and love. There is an Indian saying: "When an arrow has hit, there is no time to ask who shot it, or what kind of arrow it was." Similarly, when we encounter human suffering, we must respond with compassion rather than question the politics of those we help. Instead of asking whether their country is a friend or an enemy, we must think, "These are human beings; they are suffering, and they have a right to happiness equal to our own."

Consider, too, how many animals are being grown for slaughter, a number so great that the environment itself is being harmed. These sad facts are the result of insufficient loving care. If humanity's sense of compassion for others increased, not only would people in the world be happier, but so would the countless animals whose lives we directly affect.

A CALL FOR EDUCATION
IN COMPASSION

To increase our altruism, we must motivate ourselves to take into consideration the effects of our actions on both the present and the future. Morality, compassion, decency, and wisdom are the building blocks of all civilizations. These qualities must be cultivated in childhood, and sustained through systematic moral education in a supportive social environment, so that a more humane world may emerge. We cannot wait for the next generation to make this change; we ourselves must attempt a renewal of basic human values.

If there is any hope, it lies in future generations, but not unless we institute major change in our educational systems now. We must educate our young children in the practice of compassion on a worldwide scale. Teachers and parents can instill in children real, warmhearted human values to tremendous benefit. We need a transformation in commitment to the universal values of compassion and love.

The desperate state of our world calls us to action. Each of us has a responsibility to try to help at the deeper level of our common humanity. If with a warm heart and patience we can consider the views of others, and exchange ideas in calm discussion, we will find points of agreement. Unfortunately, humanity is too often sacrificed in defense of ideology. This is absolutely wrong. Political systems should work for the benefit of human beings, but, like money, they can control us instead of work for us.

It is our responsibility—out of love and compassion for humankind—to seek harmony among nations, ideologies, cultures, ethnic groups, and economic and political systems. As we truly come to recognize the oneness of all humankind, our motivation to find peace will grow stronger. In the deepest sense, we are really sisters and brothers, so we must share each other's suffering. Mutual respect, trust, and concern for one another's welfare is our best hope for lasting world peace.

I am convinced that despite different cultures and different political and economic systems, we are all basically the same. The more people I meet, the stronger my conviction becomes that the oneness of humanity, founded on understanding and respect, is a realistic and viable basis for our conduct. Wherever I go, this is what I speak about. I believe that the practice of compassion and love—a genuine sense of brotherhood and sisterhood—is the best universal approach. We all enjoy the feeling of being one with all humankind.

Of course, national leaders have a special responsibility in this area, but every individual must also take the initiative. Just by being human, by seeking to gain happiness and avoid suffering, you are a citizen of this planet, regardless of nationality or religious belief. We all are responsible for creating a better future.

It is not enough to issue noisy calls to halt moral degeneration; we must do something about it. Since present-day governments do not shoulder such "spiritual" responsibilities, humanitarians and religious leaders must strengthen existing civic, social, cultural, educational, and religious organizations to revive human and spiritual values. Where necessary, we must create new organizations to achieve these goals. This is our best hope for creating a more stable basis for world peace.

The seed of love and compassion is there in us instinctually, but promoting and nurturing it requires insight and education. To solve the problems humanity is facing, we need to organize meetings of scholars, educators, social workers, neuroscientists, physicians, and experts from all different fields to discuss the positive and negative effects of what we have done thus far, as well as what needs to be introduced and what needs to be changed in our educational system.

Proper environment plays a crucial role in the healthy growth of a child. All problems, including terrorism, can be overcome through education, particularly by introducing concern for others at the preschool level. Fighting, cheating, and bullying have trapped us in our present situation; now we need training in new practices to find a way out. It may seem impractical and idealistic, but we have no effective alternative except compassion, recognizing human value and the oneness of humanity: this is the only way to achieve lasting happiness.

CULTIVATING COMPASSION

All beings want happiness and do not want suffering. Living things use many different ways to remove unwanted suffering in its superficial and deep forms, but it is mostly humans who engage in techniques in the earlier part of their lives to avoid suffering later on. Both those who do and do not practice religion seek over the course of their lives to lessen some forms of suffering and to remove others, sometimes even taking on pain as a means to overcome greater suffering and gain a measure of happiness.

Everyone tries to remove superficial pain, but there is another class of techniques concerned with removing suffering on a deeper level. Spiritual practice is of this deeper type. These techniques involve an adjustment of attitude, so spiritual education basically means adjusting your thoughts in a beneficial way. This means that by adjusting counterproductive attitudes, you are *held back* from a particular kind of suffering, and are thereby freed from it. Spiritual education protects, or holds you and others back, from misery.

After first understanding your own situation and then seeking to hold yourself back from suffering, you extend your realization to other beings and develop compassion, dedicating yourself to holding others back from suffering. It makes practical sense for you, just one being, to opt for taking care of many, but by concentrating on the welfare of others, you also make yourself happier. Compassion diminishes fears about your own pain and increases your inner strength. It gives you a sense of empowerment, of being able to accomplish your tasks. It lends encouragement.

Let me give you a small example. Several years ago, when I was in Bodh Gaya, India, I fell ill from a chronic intestinal infection. On the way to the hospital, the pain in my abdomen was severe, and I was sweating a great deal. The car was passing through the area of Vulture Peak, where Buddha once taught. In general, Bihar State is poor, but this particular area is even more so. I did not even see children going to or coming from school. Just poverty. And sickness.

I have a very clear memory of a small boy with polio, who had rusty metal braces on his legs and metal crutches up to his armpits. It was obvious that he had no one to look after him. A little later on, we drove past an old man at a tea stop, wearing only a dirty piece of cloth, fallen to the ground, left to lie there with no one to take care of him.

Later, at the hospital, my thoughts kept circling on what I had seen, reflecting on how sad it was that here I had people to take care of me but those poor people had no one. That is where my thoughts went, rather than to my own suffering. In this way, though my body underwent a lot of pain (a hole had opened in my intestinal wall), my mind did not suffer any fear or discomfort. My concern was elsewhere.

If I had concentrated on my own problems, it would only have made the situation worse. When your perspective includes the suffering of limitless beings, your own suffering looks comparatively small. Compassion strengthens your outlook, and with that courage you become more relaxed.

LEARNING HOW TO RESPOND TO TROUBLE

In difficult personal circumstances, the best recourse is to try to remain as open, honest, and sincere as possible. By responding harshly or selfishly, we simply make matters worse. This is especially apparent in painful family situations. It's helpful to realize that difficult present circumstances are at least partly (if not largely) due to your own past undisciplined actions, so when you experience a difficult period, do your best to avoid behavior that will add to your burden later on. If past actions are causes of the present situation, use the present to mold a better future.

If you see that some situation or person is going to cause you harm, it is important to take action to avoid it, but once suffering has started, it should be received not as a burden, but as something that can assist you. Undergoing small sufferings in this lifetime can purify the karma of many ill deeds that you accumulated earlier. Adopting this perspective will help you realistically see the ills of this round of existence, and the more you can do this, the more you will dislike nonvirtues that lead to more such troubles.

Hardship also helps you to see the advantages of freeing yourself from negative attitudes. In addition, through your own experience of suffering you will be able to empathize with the pain of others and generate a strong desire to do something for them. So, seen in this way, suffering can provide remarkable opportunities to stimulate practice and reflection.

From this viewpoint, forces that oppose you teach inner strength, courage, and determination. This does not mean you should give in to those who would harm you. Depending on your enemy's attitude, you may have to defend yourself vigorously, but deep down try to maintain your calm by realizing that, like you, she or he is a person who wants happiness and does not want suffering. It is hard to believe, but over time, it is possible to develop such an attitude. Here is one way to do it.

Meditation

Consider the so-called enemy this way:

1. Because this person's mind is untamed, he or she engages in activities that are harmful to you.

2. If anger—the wish to harm—were part of the basic nature of this person, it could not be altered in any way, but as we have seen, hatred does not reside in the nature of a person.

3. Even if it were the nature of a person to hate, then, just as we cannot get angry at fire because it burns our hand (it is the very nature of fire to burn), so we should not get angry at a person expressing his or her nature.

4. This said, hatred is actually peripheral to a person's nature. When a cloud covers the sun we do not get angry at the sun, so we should not get angry with the so-called enemy, but instead hold the person's afflictive emotion responsible.

5. We ourselves sometimes engage in bad behavior, do we not? Still, most of us do not think of ourselves as completely bad. We should look on others the same way.

6. Therefore, the actual troublemaker is not the person, but his or her afflictive emotion.

When we lose our temper, we don't hesitate to use harsh words, even to a close friend. Afterward, when we calm down, we feel embarrassed about what happened. This indicates that we, as persons, do not really want to use such harsh words, but because we were dominated by anger, we lost our self-control.

As I mentioned earlier, we can learn to separate a corner of the mind from strong emotions like hatred and observe the mind from this vantage point; this indicates that the mind and hatred are not one, therefore the person and hatred are not one.

11

Compassion, the Road to Relief

———————

Meet adversity with a positive attitude. Keep this in mind: by greeting trouble with optimism and hope, you are undermining worse troubles down the line. Beyond that, imagine that by undergoing this problem you are easing the burden of everyone suffering problems of that kind. This constructive practice—visualizing that by accepting your pain you are compassionately using up the negative karma of everyone destined to feel such pain—is very helpful. Sometimes when I am sick, I practice taking others' suffering onto myself and giving them my potential for happiness; this gives me a good deal of mental relief.

Every day, in the early morning, I do this practice in a general way with regard to all living beings. I also single out Chinese leaders and officials who make decisions to torture or to kill particular Tibetans. I visualize them, and draw into myself their ignorance, prejudice, hatred, and pride. I feel that even if some portion of their negative attitudes came inside me, due to my own training it could not influence my behavior and turn me into a negative person. Because of this, ingesting their negativities is not that bad for me, and I view it as lessening their problems. I do this with such strong feeling that if later in the day I hear of new atrocities, although one part of my mind might get angry, the main part is still under the influence of my morning practice; the intensity of the anger quickly reduces to the point where it is groundless.

Whether this meditation really helps those officials or not, it gives me peace of mind; the personal benefit is immense. Remember, compassion is not based on agreeing with the actions of others; it is based on recognizing that we are all similar in wanting happiness and not wanting pain, even if we have silly ideas about how to achieve these goals.

MEDITATION: TAKING AND GIVING

When you see sentient beings troubled by suffering, you can make the following wish enthusiastically—from the depths of your heart—and with great force of will:

This person is suffering very badly, and despite wanting to gain happiness and alleviate suffering, does not know how to give up nonvirtues and adopt virtues. May his or her suffering, as well as its causes, ripen within me.

This is called *the practice of taking the suffering of others within yourself using the instrument of compassion*.

From the depths of your heart, you can also imagine the following:

I will give to these sentient beings without the slightest hesitation or regret whatever virtues I have accumulated in the form of good karma, which will be auspicious for them.

This is called *the practice of giving away your own happiness using the instrument of love*.

Although such mental imagining may not actually bring about the desired results, it does increase determination and willpower, while creating a peaceful atmosphere. These practices are performed in conjunction with the inhalation and exhalation of the breath—inhaling others' pain, and exhaling your own happiness into their lives.

Similarly, when you are ill or suffer an unfortunate event, imagine the following:

> May this illness or misfortune serve as a substitute for the suffering of all sentient beings.

This will keep your suffering from getting worse by fretting about it, and it will enhance your courage. It is also helpful to think:

> May the suffering that I am undergoing now function as the ripening, manifestation, and conclusion of many bad karmas that I have accumulated.

In my limited experience, these practices are great sources of inner strength and will keep a smile on your face. Worry will not help, will it?

According to Tibetan Buddhist texts on training in altruism, when you are happy, do not get too excited about it, but dedicate to the welfare of all sentient beings the good karma that yields happiness; and when you suffer, take on yourself all the pain of other sentient beings. We usually have ups and downs, but in this way you can maintain inner courage, not allowing either fortune or misfortune to disturb your peace of mind—neither too happy nor too sad, but stable.

PRACTICE IS LONG TERM

Practice is not something you do for a couple of weeks or a couple of years. Some Buddhist texts even say that enlightenment is only achieved after performing meritorious acts and developing wisdom for three periods of countless eons. If you consider this statement properly, it can encourage you to adopt a patient, persistent attitude through difficult circumstances. If learning this saddens you, this could be a good sign that you wish to achieve progress swiftly out of your great concern for others, but it could also be a sign of insufficient courage. We all need to keep in mind that transformation of inner attitudes cannot be attained without working hard at it. To believe otherwise might mean we are harboring a form of selfishness.

A gradual approach is far better than trying to jump too high too soon; otherwise, there is the great risk of trying to practice a technique for which you are not prepared. It is not easy to have an intense bond with each and every being, so do not be discouraged if biased attitudes interrupt your practice. You will need the courage to put forth an unwavering effort throughout your life and, if there are future lives, for many lifetimes to come. Such profound transformation cannot take place overnight, or in a month, or even a year. However, you will gradually notice changes in your reactions to individuals and the world. When old reactions creep back in, do not mistake this for failure, but take such incidents as prods to more practice.

If you practice sincerely, you will experience its real value. Under no circumstances should you lose hope. Hopelessness is the real cause of failure. Do not give up. If you are pessimistic, you cannot possibly succeed, so do not be discouraged. It would be very foolish to give up. You can overcome any problem. On those occasions when you feel most hopeless, you must make an especially powerful effort. We are so accustomed to faulty states of mind that it is difficult to change with just a little practice. Just a drop of something sweet cannot change a taste that is powerfully bitter. We must persist in the face of failure. If you are hopeful and determined, you will always find some measure of success.

With inner calm, even external confusion and complication will have little effect on your mind. But if your mind gives way to anger, then even when the world is peaceful and comfortable, peace of mind will elude you. There was a monk, not a great scholar, from my personal monastery who came out of Tibet to India around 1980. We knew each other, and one day we were casually chatting. He told me that while he was in a Chinese Communist gulag for almost eighteen years, he faced grave danger on a few occasions. I thought he was referring to danger to his own life, but when I asked, "What danger?" he answered, "Losing compassion toward the Chinese." During eighteen years of imprisonment and harsh treatment, he considered this the most serious threat! Most of us would feel proud to tell others about how angry we got, as if this made us some kind of hero. He knew that the real danger lay within.

You may be rich, powerful, and well educated, but without healthy feelings of kindness and compassion there will be no peace within yourself, and no peace within your family; even your children suffer. Kindness is essential to peace of mind.

Cultivating an attitude of compassion is a slow process. As you gradually internalize it day by day, and year by year, wild states of mind become less and less frequent. Like a big piece of ice in the water, your mass of problems will gradually melt away. As you transform your mind, you will transform your surroundings, since others will see the benefits of your practice of tolerance and love, and will work at bringing these practices into their own lives.

12

Compassion, Based in Equality

Since pure compassion is not biased or partial but is thoroughly imbued with equanimity, encompassing both friend and foe, such an attitude is undeniably difficult. Ordinary love and compassion are intertwined with attachment because their motivations are selfish: you care about certain people because they help you or your friends. Because such attitudes fall under the sway of attachment, they cannot be extended to enemies, only friends—your spouse, children, parents, and so forth. However, if love and compassion thrive alongside the clear recognition of the importance and rights of others, they will reach even those who would do you harm.

From childhood I have had a tendency toward love and compassion, but it was biased. When two dogs were fighting, I would have strong feelings for the one who was losing. Even when two bugs would fight, I had strong concern for the smaller one, but would be angry with the winner. That shows that my compassion was biased.

NATURE OF ATTACHMENT

Attachment increases desire, without producing any satisfaction. Consider this: there are two types of desire, unreasonable and reasonable. The first is an affliction founded on ignorance, but the second is not. To live, you need resources; therefore, desire for sufficient material things is appropriate. Such feelings as, "This is good; I want this. This is useful," are not afflictions. It is also desirable to achieve altruism, wisdom, and liberation. Indeed, all human development is born of desire.

For instance, when you have developed an affinity for all sentient beings, and desire that they all should have happiness, such desire is valid because it is unbiased. It covers *all* sentient beings. However, our present compassion, being limited to friends and family, is heavily influenced by ignorant attachment. It is biased.

Counterproductive desire involves unreasonable attachment to things. This inevitably leads to lack of contentment. This is why I said, at the beginning of this section, that attachment increases desire without producing any satisfaction. Ask yourself if you really need most of the things you want, and the answer is no. This type of desire has no limit, no way to satisfy itself. Because it leads ultimately to suffering, you must put a brake on this kind of desire.

Although in the beginning it is difficult to distinguish between reasonable and unreasonable desire, through sustained investigation and analysis you can gradually identify ignorance and the afflictive emotions, making your practice more and more pure. Attachment is one-sided, narrowly focused on yourself for just the short term; the more attached you become, the more biased and narrow you become. Even small things will disturb you. Detachment involves the absence of that kind of narrow-mindedness, but it does not mean that you have given up interest. In order to be more open-minded, more holistic, we need detachment. Its opposite, attachment, shuts things out. It is an obstacle.

The narrow-minded worldly life is characterized by what are called *the eight worldly concerns*:

   like/dislike
   gain/loss
   praise/blame
   fame/disgrace

The worldly way of life is to be unhappy when the four unfavorable ones—dislike, loss, blame, and disgrace—happen to you or your friends, but to be pleased when these happen to your enemies. This bias is based on how people act, whereas true love and compassion are based not on actions but on the crucial fact that other sentient beings want happiness and do not want suffering, just as you do, which makes everyone equal.

Some actions are positive, and some are negative, but the agents of those actions are all sentient beings with aspirations to happiness. We always need to look at things from this angle. Actions are secondary since they are sometimes positive and sometimes negative—always changing—whereas there is never any change in the fact that living beings want happiness and do not want suffering.

When a shocking event happens we instinctively react as "I," not as a Tibetan, American, European, Asian, African, or citizen of any particular nation; nor do we react as a Buddhist, or Hindu, or member of any other religious system, but just "I." This shows us the true basic human level. On that level, all of us are the same.

Little children also do not bother about religion or nationality, riches or poverty; they just want to play together. At a young age, our sense of the oneness of humanity is much fresher. As we grow older, we learn to make a lot of distinctions; a lot of secondary differences are given undue importance, and, as a result, our basic human concern diminishes. That is a problem.

Afflictive desire necessarily brings with it hatred at what opposes it, and along with that comes jealousy and all sorts of problems. Though lust itself does not harm us directly, it indirectly brings about forces that do us harm. This is why the process of expanding compassion and love begins with developing equanimity, during which the focus shifts away from whether a particular person's actions are good or bad and toward the fact that the person is the same as yourself: he or she wants happiness, not suffering. Since this desire resides in all sentient beings, your awareness of it can apply to everyone, making the basis of your concern very stable. Once you put the emphasis on their similarity with yourself, compassion has a solid foundation that does not vacillate depending on temporary circumstances.

In my own practice, when I consider, for instance, a particular person who is currently torturing Tibetans in my homeland, I do not concentrate on that person's bad attitude and bad behavior. Instead I reflect on the fact that this is a human being who, like me, wants happiness and does not want suffering; through ignorance this person is bringing pain to himself or herself and destroying their own happiness, as well as that of others. Looking at things from this perspective, my response is love and compassion. I choose that perspective, that angle. If I considered the person harming Tibetans as my enemy, I could not have compassion as my response.

Without a sense of equality, unbiased concern cannot even get started. Consider this:

1. When an intimate friend falls ill, your sense of concern, your wish that this person be freed from sickness and restored to health, is stronger than it might be for a mere acquaintance, or for someone whom you do not like. This kind of love and compassion is mixed with the desire to pursue some benefit for yourself. The person has attracted you. Your mind has exaggerated the pleasant features of that person so that desire is generated, and you feel a longing, a mixture of intimacy, and wishing to lessen whatever suffering he or she is undergoing.

2. If an attractive person with a pleasant personality loses his or her good looks or character, your readiness to sympathize with that person might disappear. But if you have a sense of compassion for an unpleasant person, then no matter how that person's character changes, the sense of compassion is not lost.

REFLECTIVE MEDITATION

Begin by noticing that within our minds we have three main categories for people—friends, neutral beings, and enemies. We may have many attitudes toward them but three of these are our main concern here: lust, indifference arising from neglect, and hatred. When any one of these three attitudes is present, it is impossible to generate a sense of closeness to all people.

Lust, hatred, and indifference must be neutralized. Here is how to do this:

1. Simultaneously visualize a friend, an enemy, and a neutral person, for whom you don't have feelings either way.

2. Examine your feelings to see who is being held closely and who is being considered at a distance.

> You feel close to your friend.
> Regarding your enemy, you feel not only distant but sometimes also anger or irritation.
> You feel nothing for the neutral person.

   Investigate why.

3. Consider whether the friend appears to be close because she or he has helped you or your friends.

4. Consider whether the enemy appears to be distant because he or she has harmed you or your friends.

5. Consider whether you feel indifference toward the neutral person because he or she has neither helped nor harmed you or your friends.

6. Realize that, like you yourself, all of these people want happiness and do not want pain, and in this important way they are all equal.

7. Remain with this realization until it sinks into the depths of your mind.

If you keep practicing with great determination, then year by year, your mind will gradually change; it will improve. This perspective will serve as a solid foundation for developing all-encompassing compassion.

A STRONG WILL

It is important to aspire to bring about the well-being of others, and to develop that desire so that it becomes stronger and stronger. This is not attachment because it is not mixed with afflictive emotions. This strong aspiration arises from detachment.

A strong ego is needed for this work, without your becoming egotistical. You need a strong will to achieve good. It is helpful to make a wish to develop a strong self in order to be able to help all beings, for a weak self could never bring your virtuous intentions to fruition. This kind of desire is reasonable and does not involve attachment. It is the one to adopt in your practice.

Unreasonable desire is to be diminished and discarded because of its narrowness.

Conclusion: Compassion, the Basis of Human Rights

It is natural and valid to have a feeling of "I," and it follows from that feeling that we want to find happiness and avoid suffering. This is our right, and it does not need further justification. All other sentient beings also wish to be free of suffering, so if you have the right to overcome suffering, then other sentient beings naturally have the same right. So what, then, is the difference between self and other? There is a great difference in number, if not in kind. Others are more numerous than you. You are just one, and the number of other sentient beings is countless.

Out of ten sick people, who does not want happiness? No one. They all want to be freed from their illness. In the practice of altruism, there is also no possible reason for an exception, for treating one person better while neglecting others. In this world alone there are billions of people, all of whom, like you, do not want suffering.

Suffering and impermanence are the nature of things. Once we recognize our community in deprivation, we see that there is no sense in being belligerent with each other. Consider a group of prisoners who are about to be executed. During their stay in prison, all of them will meet their end. There is no sense in quarrelling during their few remaining days. All of us are bound by the same nature of suffering and impermanence. Under such circumstances, there is absolutely no reason to fight with each other.

Meditative Reflection

1. Notice your natural experience of "I," as in "I want this," "I do not want that."
2. Recognize that it is natural to want happiness and to not want pain. This is valid, and does not require further justification.
3. Based on this natural desire, you have the right to obtain happiness and to get rid of suffering.
4. Just as you have this right, so do others, and in equal measure.
5. Consider the fact that the difference between yourself and others is only that you are just one single person, whereas there are countless other living beings on this planet alone.

6. Pose this question: Should I use every living being to attain my happiness, or should I help others gain happiness?

7. Imagine yourself, calm and reasonable, looking to your right at another version of yourself—but this self is overly proud, never thinking of the welfare of others, concerned only with his or her own self.

8. On your left visualize a number of destitute people unrelated to you, needy and in pain.

9. You, in the middle, are an unbiased, sensible person. Consider that those people on both sides of you want happiness and want to get rid of pain; in this way, they are equal, the same.

10. But think:

> The selfishly motivated person on the right is just one person, whereas the others are far greater in number. Which side is more important, the one with the single, self-centered person, or the vast group of poor, helpless people?

> To which side will you devote your energies? As the unbiased person in the middle, you will naturally favor the greater number of suffering people.

11. Reflect on this thought:

> If I, as just one person, take advantage of the many, it would be truly contrary to my humanity, and to common sense. To sacrifice a lot for the sake of a little is foolish.

12. Thinking this way, you will decide:

> I am going to direct my energies to the many rather than to this one selfish person.

For me, this meditation is particularly effective. It makes very clear the foolishness of choosing a life of egotism and self-cherishing. You can understand the principles of this meditation from your own experience—that self-cherishing leads to ill deeds such as stealing, sexual misconduct, lying, divisive talk, harsh speech, gossip, and even murder, and that other-cherishing does not.

With this meditation you can learn to cherish others. Remember that you cherish yourself naturally, not out of any sense that you have been kind to yourself. It is the very fact that you cherish your life that leads you to want to get rid of suffering and gain happiness, just as all sentient beings do. Even if you could use all other beings for your own aims, you would not be happy. But if you, just one being, serve others as fully as you can, this endeavor will be a source of inner joy.

It is easy to understand that you will lose out if you neglect everyone else by overemphasizing yourself, and that you will gain greatly from valuing others as you cherish yourself. These facts are confirmed by our own experience.

Cherishing others makes a huge difference in the strength of our motivation to restrain from ill deeds, such as killing. Because altruistic people consider another's life to be as important as their own, they avoid ill deeds out of a desire to protect the other person. The same is true for stealing, adultery, lying, divisive talk, harsh speech, and even senseless chatter. In this way, altruistic people eliminate the causes of trouble in the future. When you are concerned about others, your own welfare is fulfilled automatically.

Take these reflections to heart, and you will gradually become less selfish and have more respect for others. With such an attitude, real love and compassion can grow.

LIMITLESS MERIT FROM LIMITLESS COMPASSION

Even if your motivation to be altruistic is modest, acting on it will definitely give you a degree of mental peace.

Generating concern for others has vast power to transform your mind, even though it is incremental. When you practice compassion for the sake of all living beings—including animals—then that same degree of limitless merit will accrue to you.

Truly altruistic people have concern for limitless numbers of sentient beings without any consideration of friend or foe, nationality or ethnic group, and this compassion extends to each and every type of suffering. Such altruistic people want to establish others in a state of happiness endowed with all possible favorable qualities. To become able to help on such a vast scale, they are willing to practice in order to develop their own abilities to help with effort like invisible armor, impervious to impatience and discouragement. Since their perspective is so vast, they accrue meritorious positive karma through whatever they are doing, developing power for good as limitless as the number of beings to whom they have dedicated themselves.

When you consider the vast scope of this task, you might become discouraged and shrink from it. However, since the sentient beings that are the recipients of your love and compassion are limitless in number, the beneficial forces accumulated by your altruistic attitude are also limitless. Looking at it this way, you will see that transformation is indeed possible, which will keep you from laziness and procrastination. Spiritual transformation becomes realistic when you consider the effectiveness of love, compassion, and altruism. They will support you on your path, and you will be amazed at their power.

Other-concern also puts your own situation in perspective. At one point I was particularly saddened about the situation of Tibet, but then I remembered that I had taken vows to be altruistic, and indeed every day I had frequently reflected on the prayer:

> As long as the sky exists
> And as long as there are sentient beings,
> May I remain to help
> Relieve them of all their pain.

As soon as I remembered this, the feeling of a heavy burden fell away, much like heavy clothes being lifted off me. Boundless altruistic commitment relieves the specific causes of dejection by placing them in a broader perspective, where it becomes clear that they are not worthy. Just as a narrow perspective makes even a small problem unbearable, being concerned for all sentient beings widens your view, making you more realistic. In this way, an altruistic attitude helps to reduce your own pain right now.

ONE FAMILY

In a sense, all human beings belong to a single family. We need to embrace the oneness of humanity and show concern for everyone—not just *my* family or *my* country or *my* continent. We must show concern for every being, not just the few that resemble us most. Differences of religion, ideology, race, economic system, social system, and government are all secondary.

First, you need to realize that each and every other sentient being wants happiness and does not want suffering, just as you do; in this fundamental way you and they are equal. Then, when you consider that you are only a single person measured against an infinite number of other sentient beings, you realize that it would be completely ridiculous either to neglect the welfare of others, or to use them for the sake of your own pleasure. It would be far more reasonable to dedicate yourself to their service.

When you consider the situation this way, it becomes very clear. No matter how important you may be, you are only a single person. To lose the happiness of a single person is important, but not so important as losing the happiness of many other beings.

BECOMING AWARE OF
UNINTENDED KINDNESS

To deepen your gratitude toward all people, it is helpful to reflect on the unintended kindness of those who provide goods and services without even knowing the names or faces of those whom they serve. All of us are dependent on people who have no special motivation to help us individually.

If we want a grove of trees to roam in, we are happy to have a park, and we value it even though the stand of trees itself has no motivation to help. In much the same way, when sentient beings provide necessities for your life, they are helping you in particular without ever knowing you in particular. In this life so many facilities we enjoy—buildings, roads, shops, and so forth—are produced by other people. As you can see, thousands of people in this lifetime, whom you may never meet, are showing you kindness.

Contemplation

Here are some sample contemplations:

1. Think of all the food in a supermarket and of all the people involved in making it available—from the

farmers to the truckers to the people who put it out
on the shelves.

2. Realize that even a glass of water depends on a vast
nexus of individuals.

3. Consider that all the facilities we use—buildings,
roads, tunnels, bridges, buses, cars, and so forth—
are produced by other people.

Providing services is a form of kindness, of nurturing,
no matter what the motivation may be. When you experience this nexus of kindness in a deep way, it becomes
possible to extend this appreciation even to those you do
not know.

Human society exists because it is impossible to live
in complete isolation. When you gain more appreciation both for the motivated kindnesses bestowed on you
by friends and others and for the unintended kindnesses
provided to you each day, you will naturally contribute to
a healthier society. Without the appreciation of kindness,
society breaks down. As I said earlier, as small children
we very much depend on the kindness of our parents, and
again in old age we depend on the kindness of others, but
between childhood and old age we falsely believe we are
independent, whereas this is not so.

We are interdependent by nature, and since we must

live together, we should do so with a positive attitude of concern for one another. The aim of human society must be the compassionate betterment of all from one moment to the next.

MY FINAL ADVICE

Each one of us is responsible for all of humankind. We need to think of each other as true sisters and brothers, and to be concerned with each other's welfare. We must seek to lessen the suffering of others. Rather than working solely to acquire wealth, we need to do something meaningful, something seriously directed toward the welfare of humanity as a whole.

If, in the midst of the garbage of lust, hatred, and ignorance—emotions that afflict our own minds and our world—we generate a compassionate attitude, we should cherish this like a jewel. This precious discovery can give us happiness and real tranquility. Alternatives such as taking a vacation or drugs only bring temporary relief. A disciplined attitude of true other-concern, in which you cherish others more than yourself, is helpful both to you and to them. And it does no harm to anyone, temporarily or in the long run. Compassion is a priceless jewel.

Care about others at all times. Practices for training

the mind can be summed up in two sentences: "If you are able, you should help others. If you are not able, you should at least not harm others." Both are based on love and compassion. First, you must gain control over the tendency to do harm, voluntarily restraining your hurtful physical and verbal actions. The next level begins when you can bring these destructive factors somewhat under your control, giving you a better chance to help others. Altruism is the spirit out of which we choose to take action that brings happiness to others. Even a small experience of altruism brings a measure of mental peace right away.

This sequence means that if you cannot help others, do no harm. This is the essential meaning of the practice of transformation of mind and heart. This is my simple religion. No need for temples. No need for complicated philosophy. Your own mind, your own heart is the temple; the philosophy is simple kindness.

My earnest request is that you practice compassion whether you believe in a religion or not. Through this practice, you will come to realize the value of compassion for your own peace of mind. The very atmosphere of your own life becomes happier, which promotes good health, perhaps even a longer life. By developing a warm heart, we can also transform others. As we become nicer human beings, our neighbors, friends, parents, spouses, and children experience less anger. They will become more warmhearted, compassionate, and harmonious. You will see the world around you change little by little. Even a small act of compassion grants meaning and purpose to our lives.

Review of the Exercises

How to Regard Anger

1. If a person shows anger to you, and you show anger in return, the result is a disaster.

2. However, if you control your anger and show its opposite—love, compassion, tolerance, and patience—then not only do you remain in peace, but gradually the anger of others also will diminish.

3. Anger may lead to temporary success, yielding a little satisfaction for a brief period, but ultimately will cause further difficulties.

4. When someone tries to take advantage of you, first you must clearly understand that this person is a human being, and has a right to be happy.

5. Then, you can act according to the circumstances he or she has created, responding strongly if neces-

sary, but never losing your compassionate perspective.

Compassion is the key.

How to Appreciate Enemies

1. Consider that in order to build character, the practice of patience is essential.
2. See that the best way to practice patience requires an enemy.
3. Understand that in this way enemies are very valuable for the opportunities they provide.
4. Decide that instead of getting angry with those who block your wishes, you will inwardly respond with gratitude.

By seeing things this way, you can change your attitude toward adversity. This is very difficult, but very rewarding. By considering the matter deeply, you will see that even great enemies who intend you serious harm are also, in a sense, extending great kindness to you. For only when faced with the work of enemies can you learn real inner strength.

How to Reflect on Change

Examine your feelings to see who is being held closely and who is being considered at a distance. Investigate the matter this way:

> You naturally feel close to your friend; regarding your enemy, you feel not only distant but sometimes anger or irritation; you feel nothing for a neutral person. However, it is by no means certain that a friend, an enemy, or a neutral person will at all times either help, harm, or do neither. When you are generating negative thoughts, and negative feelings such as hatred or anger, even a friend is seen as an enemy, and when negative thoughts toward an enemy disappear, the enemy becomes a friend.

By reflecting in these ways, you can loosen the hold that afflictive emotions like anger and hatred have on you.

Watching How You Get into Trouble

1. Visualize and allow yourself to feel a time when you were filled with hatred or lust.

2. Does it not seem that the hated or desired person or thing is extremely substantial, very concrete?

3. Is there a conflict between appearance and reality? Notice how you:

First perceive the object;

Then determine if the object is good or bad;

Then conclude that the object's goodness or badness exists inherently in the object;

Then generate lust or hatred according to whether the object's goodness or badness has been exaggerated.

Considering How Phenomena Appear in an Intense Situation

1. Remember a time when you felt intense hatred or lust. The hated or desired person or thing seemed extremely substantial, didn't it?

2. When you reflect on how things appeared to you in such an intense situation, you will find that they seemed to exist in their own right.

3. However, the fact is that nothing exists in this way; everything is set up in dependence on its causes, its parts, and on the way we perceive it.

4. When you notice your own exaggerated reactions, you will see that you have lost sight of the fact that people and things are dependent on an interrelated web of factors and conditions.

5. Keep trying to see and feel how your focus narrows in intense situations of lust and anger. When you notice this confinement, you will naturally want to loosen the bonds of the exaggerated emotions that keep you there.

How to Deflate Attachment by Being Aware of Impermanence

Contemplate things this way:

1. It is certain that I will die. Death cannot be avoided. My lifetime is running out and cannot be extended.

2. When I will die is unknown. Human lifespan varies. The causes of death are many, and the causes of life comparatively few. The body is fragile.

3. We are all in this same tenuous situation, so there is no point in quarrelling and fighting, or wasting all our mental and physical energy on accumulating money and property.

4. By mistaking what deteriorates moment by mo-

ment for something constant, I bring pain upon myself as well as others. I should reduce my attachment to passing fancies.

5. From the depths of my heart, I should seek to get beyond these cycles of suffering created by mistaking what is fleeting for permanent.

6. In the long run, what helps most is my transformed attitude.

Being aware of impermanence calls for discipline—taming the mind—but this does not mean punishment, or control from the outside. Discipline does not mean prohibition; rather, it means that when there is a contradiction between short-term and long-term interests, you sacrifice the former for the latter. This is *self*-discipline, which is based on understanding the cause and effect of one's own actions. This type of discipline offers protection.

How to Meditatively Reflect on the Disadvantages of Anger

1. *Anger creates havoc*

Anger motivates rude words and harsh physical actions, immediately creating an unpleasant atmosphere. Anger diminishes your power to distinguish right from wrong, an ability that is one of the highest human attributes. When it is lost, we are lost. Sometimes, it is necessary to respond strongly, but this can be done without anger. Anger is not necessary. It has no value.

2. *Anger magnifies problems*

Even small actions can lead to huge effects, just as a small seed can give rise to a great tree. For instance, uttering an ugly name to describe another person while motivated by anger can have rippling effects far into the future.

3. *Anger undermines virtues*

The ability of a virtuous deed to generate a good effect can be undermined by strong anger, which makes it doubly important to control your rage. If, after you performed a virtuous action and accumulated its potential, the potential benefit of that good deed remained intact without diminishing until its positive fruit issued forth, the situation would not be so tenuous, but that is not the case. Instead, the effect of a strong nonvirtuous state of mind, such as anger, overpowers the potential future benefit of a virtuous act so that it cannot issue forth, much like scorching a seed.

Conversely, a strong virtuous attitude overpowers the negative potential established by misdeeds, making them unable to issue *their* effects. Therefore, it is necessary not only to take many actions that will set in motion future good effects, but also to avoid setting in motion negative forces that would undercut the future benefit of the good you are doing.

As you analyze this situation more and more, gradually your convictions about the uselessness of anger will strengthen. Repeated reflection on the disadvantages of anger will cause you to realize that it is senseless, even pathetic. When it becomes obvious that the effects of anger are harmful, you will arrive at the conclusion that there are no positive results to be found in anger, hatred, and violence. This decision will cause you to be less and less willing to acquiesce to negativity.

Maintaining Introspection

1. Since the mind is drawn into lust for pleasant objects and into hatred for the unpleasant, it is important to control your senses by keeping away, if possible, from those places where such destructive emotions are generated.

2. At those times when your senses encounter pleasant and unpleasant objects, practice keeping your mind from falling into lust and hatred.

3. Identify both lust and hatred as self-destructive emotions by recognizing their disadvantages; determine not to sanction them.

4. Mindful that these emotions need to be restrained, use introspection to see whether you are encountering objects and situations that might generate self-destructive emotions. When such objects and situations are present, see if afflictive emotions are actually being generated.

You need to keep this up no matter what you are doing. In this way, you can make use of each day of your life, while recognizing that lust and hatred continue to arise intermittently.

Examining Seemingly Solid Appearances

You are getting angry because someone has harmed, is harming, or will harm you, your family, or your friend. In that flash of rage, you feel that both the subject (I), and the object (the enemy), are tangible, independent entities. Because you mistakenly accept the appearance of things, anger is generated. Therefore, at or even before that first flash of rage make use of reason to examine:

Who am I?
Who is this one who is being hurt?
What is the enemy?
Is the enemy the body of this other person?
Is the enemy his or her mind?

If you examine things in this way, the enemy who previously seemed to be created in and of herself or himself as something to get angry at, and this "I" who was inherently created to be hurt, seem to disappear. And the anger breaks apart.

How to Avoid Getting Bogged Down in Appearances

Try viewing phenomena as like illusions this way:

1. The reflection of a face is undeniably produced in dependence on a face and a mirror, and is empty of the eyes, ears, and other features it appears to have.

2. The reflection of a face undeniably disappears when either face or mirror is absent.

3. Similarly, even though a person does not have even a speck of independent existence, it is not contradictory for a person to perform actions and to experience the effects of those actions.

Because lust and hatred stem from our accepting the appearance of inflated qualities—good or bad—the practice of seeing people and things as being like an illusion, like a show with a false facade, helps reduce unfavorable emotions.

Undermining Afflictive Emotions by Knowing the Nature of the Mind

It is very helpful each day to identify the nature of the mind and concentrate on it. However, it is difficult to catch hold of the mind, hidden as it is beneath our own scattered thoughts. As a technique to identify the basic nature of the mind:

1. First stop remembering what happened in the past.
2. Then stop thinking about what might happen in the future.
3. Let the mind flow of its own accord without the overlay of thought. Observe it for a while in its natural state.

Between the time of hearing a noise and identifying its source, you can sense a state of mind devoid of thought but not asleep, in which the object is a reflection of the mind's luminous knowing. At such a time you can grasp the basic nature of the mind. In the beginning, when you are not used to this practice, it is quite difficult, but in time the mind appears like clear water. Try to stay with this state of mind without being distracted by thoughts, and become accustomed to it. Practice this meditation in the early morning, when your mind has awakened and is clear, but your senses are not yet fully engaged.

Responding to Trouble

Consider the so-called enemy:

1. Because this person's mind is untamed, he or she engages in activities that are harmful to you.
2. If anger—the wish to harm—were part of the basic nature of this person, it could not be altered in any way, but as we have seen, hatred does not reside in the nature of a person.
3. Even if it were the nature of a person to hate, then just as we cannot get angry at fire because it burns our hand (it is the very nature of fire to burn), so we should not get angry at a person expressing his or her nature.
4. This said, hatred is actually peripheral to a person's nature. When a cloud covers the sun we do not get angry at the sun, so we should not get angry with the so-called enemy, but instead hold the person's afflictive emotion responsible.
5. We ourselves sometimes engage in bad behavior, do we not? Still, most of us do not think of our-

selves as completely bad. We should look on others the same way.

6. Therefore, the actual troublemaker is not the person, but his or her afflictive emotion.

When we lose our temper, we don't hesitate to use harsh words, even to a close friend. Afterward, when we calm down, we feel embarrassed about what happened. This indicates that we, as persons, do not really want to use such harsh words, but because we were dominated by anger, we lost our self-control.

Compassionately Relieving Pain and Lovingly Giving Happiness

1. When you see sentient beings troubled by suffering, you can make the following wish enthusiastically— from the depths of your heart—and with great force of will:

This person is suffering very badly, and despite wanting to gain happiness and alleviate suffering, does not know how to give up nonvirtues and adopt virtues. May his or her suffering, as well as its causes, ripen within me.

This is called *the practice of taking the suffering of others within yourself using the instrument of compassion.*

2. From the depths of your heart you can also imagine the following:

> I will give to these sentient beings without the slightest hesitation or regret whatever virtues I have accumulated in the form of good karma, which will be auspicious for them.

This is called *the practice of giving away your own happiness using the instrument of love.*

Although such mental imagining may not actually bring about the desired results, it does increase determination and will power, while creating a peaceful atmosphere. These practices are performed in conjunction with the inhalation and exhalation of the breath—inhaling others' pain, and exhaling your own happiness into their lives.

3. Similarly, when you are ill, or suffer an unfortunate event, imagine the following:

> May this illness or misfortune serve as a substitute for the suffering of all sentient beings.

This will keep your suffering from getting worse by fretting about it, and it will enhance your courage. It is also helpful to think:

> May the suffering that I am undergoing now function as the ripening, manifestation, and conclusion of many bad karmas that I have accumulated.

According to Tibetan Buddhist texts on training in altruism, when you are happy, do not get too excited about it, but dedicate to the welfare of all sentient beings the good karma that yields happiness; and when you suffer, take on yourself all the pain of other sentient beings. We usually have ups and downs, but in this way you can maintain inner courage, not allowing either fortune or misfortune to disturb your peace of mind—neither too happy nor too sad, but stable.

How to Develop a Strong Feeling of Equality

Begin by noticing that within our minds we have three main categories for people—friends, neutral beings, and enemies. We may have many attitudes toward them but three of these are our main concern here: lust, indifference arising from neglect, and hatred. When any one of these three attitudes is present, it is impossible to generate a sense of closeness to all people. Lust, hatred, and indifference must be neutralized. Here is how to do this:

1. Simultaneously visualize a friend, an enemy, and a neutral person, for whom you don't have feelings either way.

2. Examine your feelings to see who is being held closely and who is being considered at a distance.

> You feel close to your friend.
> Regarding your enemy, you feel not only distant but sometimes also anger or irritation.
> You feel nothing for the neutral person.

Investigate why.

3. Consider whether the friend appears to be close because she or he has helped you or your friends.

4. Consider whether the enemy appears to be distant because he or she has harmed you or your friends.

5. Consider whether you feel indifference toward the neutral person because he or she has neither helped nor harmed you or your friends.

6. Realize that, like you yourself, all of these people want happiness and do not want pain, and in this important way they are all equal.

7. Remain with this realization until it sinks into the depths of your mind.

If you keep practicing with great determination, then year by year, your mind will gradually change; it will improve. This perspective will serve as a solid foundation for developing all-encompassing compassion.

How to Recognize Global Human Rights

1. Notice your natural experience of "I," as in "I want this," "I do not want that."

2. Recognize that it is natural to want happiness and to not want pain. This is valid, and does not require further justification.

3. Based on this natural desire, you have the right to obtain happiness and to get rid of suffering.

4. Just as you have this right, so do others, and in equal measure.

5. Consider the fact that the difference between yourself and others is only that you are just one

single person, whereas there are countless other living beings on this planet alone.

6. Pose this question: Should I use every living being to attain my happiness, or should I help others gain happiness?

7. Imagine yourself, calm and reasonable, looking to your right at another version of yourself—but this self is overly proud, never thinking of the welfare of others, concerned only with his or her own self.

8. On your left, visualize a number of destitute people unrelated to you, needy and in pain.

9. You, in the middle, are an unbiased, sensible person. Consider that those people on both sides of you want happiness and want to get rid of pain; in this way, they are equal, the same.

10. But think:

> The selfishly motivated person on the right is just one person, whereas the others are far greater in number. Which side is more important, the one with the single, self-centered person, or the vast group of poor, helpless people?

To which side will you devote your energies? As the unbiased person in the middle, you will naturally favor the greater number of suffering people.

11. Reflect on this thought:

> If I, as just one person, take advantage of the many, it would be truly contrary to my humanity, and to common sense. To sacrifice a lot for the sake of a little is foolish.

12. Thinking this way, you will decide:

> I am going to direct my energies to the many rather than to this one selfish person.

Recognizing Kindness

Here are some sample contemplations:

1. Think of all the food in a supermarket and of all the people involved in making it available—from the farmers to the truckers to the people who put it on the shelves.
2. Realize that even a glass of water depends on a vast nexus of individuals.
3. Consider that all the facilities we use—buildings,

roads, tunnels, bridges, buses, cars, and so forth—
are produced by other people.

Providing services is a form of kindness, of nurturing,
no matter what the motivation may be. When you experience this nexus of kindness in a deep way, it becomes
possible to extend this appreciation even to those you do
not know.

It is very clear that all of the troubles on this earth are ultimately due to egoism and self-cherishing. Remember that
you cherish yourself naturally, not out of any sense that
you have been kind to yourself. From the very fact that you
cherish your life you want to get rid of suffering and gain
happiness. In the same way, all sentient beings naturally
cherish themselves, and from this they want to get rid of
suffering and gain happiness. We are all the same; the difference is that others are many, whereas you are just one
person. Even if you could use all other beings for your
own aims, you would not be happy. But if you, just one being, serve others as fully as you can, this endeavor will be a
source of inner joy.

Selected Readings

His Holiness the Dalai Lama, Tenzin Gyatso. *Becoming Enlightened*. Translated and edited by Jeffrey Hopkins. New York: Atria Books/Simon & Schuster, 2009.

—. *How to Expand Love: Widening the Circle of Loving Relationships*. Translated and edited by Jeffrey Hopkins. New York: Atria Books/Simon & Schuster, 2005.

—. *How to Practice: The Way to a Meaningful Life*. Translated and edited by Jeffrey Hopkins. New York: Atria Books/Simon & Schuster, 2002.

—. *How to See Yourself as You Really Are*. Translated and edited by Jeffrey Hopkins. New York: Atria Books/ Simon & Schuster, 2006.

—. *Kindness, Clarity, and Insight*. Translated and edited by Jeffrey Hopkins; coedited by Elizabeth Napper.

Ithaca, NY: Snow Lion Publications, 1984; revised edition, 2006.

—. *Mind of Clear Light: Advice on Living Well and Dying Consciously.* Translated and edited by Jeffrey Hopkins. New York: Atria Books/Simon & Schuster, 2002.

—. *The Meaning of Life: Buddhist Perspectives on Cause and Effect.* Translated and edited by Jeffrey Hopkins. Boston: Wisdom Publications, 2000.

Hopkins, Jeffrey. *A Truthful Heart: Buddhist Practices for Connecting with Others.* Ithaca, NY: Snow Lion Publications, 2008.

—. *Nagarjuna's Precious Garland: Buddhist Advice for Living and Liberation.* Ithaca, NY: Snow Lion Publications, 1998.

Rinchen, Geshe Sonam and Ruth Sonam. *Yogic Deeds of Bodhisattvas: Gyel-tsap on Aryadeva's Four Hundred.* Ithaca, NY: Snow Lion Publications, 1994.

Tsongkhapa, *The Great Treatise on the Stages of the Path to Enlightenment,* vols. 1–3, trans. and ed. Joshua W. C. Cutler and Guy Newland. Ithaca, NY: Snow Lion Publications, 2000 and 2003.

Wallace, Vesna A., and B. Alan Wallace. *A Guide to the Bodhisattva Way of Life*. Ithaca, NY: Snow Lion Publications, 1997.